Advance Praise for *Hope for Troubled Minds*

Kathy Day

As senior family resource and advocacy manager for Treatment Advocacy Center, I am honored to have been allowed to read and review *Hope for Troubled Minds*. Tony Roberts has compiled a comprehensive anthology of stories and letters from families across the country, humanizing mental illness. The people who suffer are not only our loved ones who are ill, but also the families of these loved ones. These poignant tributes are heartfelt—sometimes tragic and sad, but sometimes uplifting. These stories are about humans trying to find their way through the maze of mental healthcare.

In my work, I interact with families across the country who are struggling to find help for their loved ones or themselves. The system of care is very difficult to navigate, especially while simultaneously trying to find the treatment and services our loved ones so desperately need. When they can't find proper services, or lack the insight to realize they need help, we are the ones who navigate the system of care for them.

The stories in this book demonstrate the love and support these families provide to very ill loved ones. We celebrate the smallest of successes, because we recognize the difficult daily challenges confronting them due to a no-fault brain illness. We recognize their needs and limitations, always encouraging them to do more.

The families who are bravely sharing their stories and their love for their children, spouses, siblings, parents, and friends are the true heroes of serious mental illness.

Their stories demonstrate the dedication of families to supporting their loved ones and to managing their illnesses when unprepared to do so and lacking professional support from the clinical teams, law enforcement, or the courts.

There are quotes that stand out for me:

"There is not a destination. There will be pit-stops, rest areas, traffic jams, overnight stays away from home, flat tires, engine troubles, but he will never be alone. Landon has an amazing family and support system in place and when you are traveling a journey such as a severe mental illness, family and support are priceless."

". . . dealing with humans was much harder. No one can understand the amount of energy and patience and courage it takes to get through one day with mental illness."

"Your illness has helped me to become a more compassionate and nonjudgmental person. I no longer take anything for granted and appreciate the small things in life—a sunny day, the sounds of waves crashing, or a moment that makes me laugh. A day without chaos is truly a blessing."

"I was actually relieved when you were in jail, because at least I knew where you were, I could visit you, and you weren't homeless."

Whether you have a loved one who is diagnosed with a serious mental illness, or you want to learn more about the topic and those who provide care, this book is for you. It's important to know about this subset of people who struggle in the shadows due to an invisible illness that can strike anyone. We need to talk about it openly and share our stories widely.

Kathy Day *is the senior family resources and advocacy manager for Treatment Advocacy Center. She also has a family member with severe mental illness.*

HOPE FOR
TROUBLED MINDS

TRIBUTES TO THOSE WITH BRAIN ILLNESSES
AND THEIR LOVED ONES

Tony Roberts & Contributors

A Way With Words Publishing
Columbus, IN
©2023 Delight in Disorder Ministries

Editor's Note: The letters, poems, and songs in this publication reflect the personal views and perspectives of their writers. Any language pertaining to God, mental health diagnoses, and treatments has been left in its original wording to preserve the vulnerability and honesty of the writers to their loved ones. The language used is not intended to teach, diagnose, treat, or convey a specific view to the reader regarding spiritual, mental, or physical health.

Chief Editor: Tony Roberts
Associate Editor: Katie R. Dale
Line-Item Editor: Janet Coburn
Book Cover Design: Katie R. Dale
Interior Formatting: Leanne Sype

Hardback ISBN: 978-1-7350617-1-9
eBook ISBN: 978-1-7350617-2-6

Dedicated to the family and person of James Mark Rippee and all families represented in this book and beyond who bravely battle brain illness.

Until We Are Reunited
by Catherine Rippee Hanson

My sister and I thought we were strong.
Though burdened with a heavy wrong.
We lost our brother to injury and disease,
Leaving us with bittersweet memories.

We tried to fix it, to make it right.
So much love and hope in sight;
But darkness would not be denied.
And his life . . . the world would not abide.

Schizophrenia . . . was his last undoing.
Making his world wild and confusing;
And though we tried to keep him safe,
He turned away, lost in life's dark maze.

Homelessness was his final fate.
The streets . . . his home; there's no debate.
Our hearts were broken, tears were shed.
Before the end when he was dead.

Our brother's death is sad and tragic.
A simple illness, but too late for magic.
His soul departed from this world.
Leaving us unraveled, thoughts unfurled.

We grieved in sadness; we kept some hope.

Remembering our brother, trying to cope.
We clung to hope, as a beacon of light;
In honor of our brother, each day and night.

He had a life of love and a life of pain.
The bravery of his journey we'll sustain.
From his shining light, we'll never be apart.

For he will always be with us in our hearts.
We will keep on honoring him and his memory.
Until we are all reunited in eternity.

Table of Contents

Editor's Note

I began this project in early 2021. I first envisioned it to be a collection of interviews I conducted and then summarized in narrative form. I started conducting interviews and wound up canceling more than I kept; living with rapid cycling bipolar disorder is not conducive to keeping a schedule.

After a few months of bemoaning my fate, my wife and muse inspired me with the idea of having people submit tribute letters to their loved ones caring for them as they lived with brain illness (especially schizophrenia, bipolar, schizoaffective disorder, and major clinical depression). After a couple of these, I thought it would be nice to offer loved ones a chance to write about the people with brain illness. Sort of love "in spite of." Often those of us diagnosed get the most compassion and it's our loved ones who have it the hardest.

About 20 of these tributes appeared first in my blog, delightindisorder.org (now the website for our nonprofit Delight in Disorder Ministries). Katie R. Dale agreed to be Associate Editor, and this book would not be possible without her wise counsel. This also goes for Adela Dickey, our webmaster. Janet Coburn did a thorough and thoughtful job on the line editing. Leanne Sype formatted the book. And Laura Pogliano spread the word on social media.

Just a word about the contents: if anyone submitted something that is not included, I am directly responsible. We sought out diversity, but some voices are not represented that much (such as fathers, as Ron Powers points out in his gracious Foreword). It is our hope that publishing this collection might spark fathers and others not represented to submit a tribute for a potential later work. (You can send your submissions directly to me via tony@delightindisorder.org.)

Finally, we are delighted to share that all net proceeds from the sale of this book will be evenly distributed to three vital mental health causes: the National Alliance on Mental Illness (NAMI), the Treatment Advocacy Center (TAC), and Delight in Disorder Ministries (DiDMin).

When I was in college, I wrote a novella called *Life (in Obvious Places)*. The thinly veiled main character is asked by a young woman named Claudia, "Why don't you write any love stories?" He replies, "I don't know any."

This is a love story I now know very well.

–Tony E. Roberts

Foreword

Not Just "Worthy," but Essential
Ron Powers

I'll begin with a disclosure: I coursed through my first reading of *Hope for Troubled Minds* on a wave of doubt. I wondered whether I was the right person to write a Foreword to it. I wondered whether anyone was. I wondered whether a Foreword could be at once truthful and supportive of the contents.

Hope for Troubled Minds, after all, is a book that deals with mental illness, a catastrophic affliction known for its propensity to crush hope.

I frankly winced as I came across passages such as, "Through these years, God has taught me many valuable lessons and initiated growth and maturity in myself—sometimes against my will."

And, "I waited until the sky was/perfect blue with billowy clouds/then plucked a cloud just right for you/to rest upon."

And, "I went to Catholic schools and like to think he is 'up there.'"

And: ". . . with God's help we will work things out."

I am no enemy of religious believers. I respect them. Through my childhood and college years, and at intervals beyond, church membership was a part of my life. Yet the skepticism—the doubt—that eventually took hold in me has led me to wonder why God may or may not be in the mood to help. And why God selects some for his blessing and seems to ignore others, many others. And why God chose to plague mankind with mental illness in the first place.

"Dang!" I (more or less) exclaimed at some point. "Am I in the right book here?"

A "valuable lesson"? Mental illness is a dreadful and dreaded curse. It competes with cancer for the distinction of what one writer has called "The Emperor of All Maladies."

What does this desolate truth have to do with plucking billowy clouds from perfect blue skies?

Yet I paged on.

Hope for Troubled Minds is a collection of letters and internet posts, most of them written by wives and mothers to husbands, parents, sons, and daughters whose lives were invaded by the worst of the worst, those rare strains of madness for which there is yet no cure: schizophrenia, Bipolar disorder, Schizoaffective disorder, and one or two other closely related afflictions.

Serious mental illness (SMI) is a disease apart, even from "ordinary" mental illness. Many people, in fact, reject the term in favor of "brain disease," claiming there is really nothing "mental" about SMI.

Mental connotes the abstract mind: the capacity to think, to reason, to move the body purposefully. The mind can be happy or sad or angry or depressed or joyful or alienated, depending upon what is going on with an individual. It is a semi-metaphoric concept.

There is nothing metaphoric about the brain. The brain is a thing: the physical engine of the physical body. With its nearly infinite system of lobes, neurons (around 86 billion total), cells, chemicals, neurotransmitters, axons, glands, ganglia, and other materials, the human brain is a three-pound galaxy of furious activity. When all its components are functioning as they should, the brain can usually withstand the transient storms of emotion and even addiction.

In rare cases—estimates range from two to nearly five brains in a hundred—the engine fails. This is due to flawed, inherited genes; nearly everyone has some. Sometimes these bad genes flow together and form a devastating cocktail in spaces where the adolescent brain is "pruning" itself of used-up neurons. This cocktail, especially if it is reinforced by severe trauma, the pressures of overpopulation, air pollution, even (it is thought by some neuropsychiatrists) pesticides and cat fur, can disrupt the essential neurotransmitters dopamine and serotonin.

When this happens, the damage is permanent, and reason fails. Thus SMI stems not from mere anger or depression or social alienation or addiction, but from the very brain chemicals that its victims are born with: the destructive cocktail of flawed neurons that can flow together around mid-adolescence, when the brain is pruning its old cells and waiting for new ones to form.

This rare imbalance can play havoc with rational thought and behavior; cause delusions and hallucinations; and, if the victim remains untreated, trigger violent behavior to others or to the self. Stabilization of the victim is possible through a carefully prescribed, lifetime regimen of antipsychotic medication combined with therapy and a loving environment.

If you have bought this book or are deciding whether to buy it—or if you yourself are among the afflicted—chances are that you know at least some of these things.

Chances also are that you're a little like me: doubtful about any book about SMI that has the word "hope" in its title. On hyper-alert when billowy clouds and perfect blue skies pop up in the pages.

As you may have guessed by now, I am a citizen of the Sub-Nation of Crazy People and their kin. I belong to "and their kin." It's a mostly dismal and wary realm. We citizens share some bleak cultural traits: bewilderment and dismay over what has invaded and distorted our lives; fear, fury, and frustration at the larger world's clueless indifference; deep and painful and permanent loss.

We are Job's sons and daughters.

And we are hyper-sensitive to phoniness. We shrink back from well-meaning friends' cheery How-Are-Yous—especially when we know that those friends really don't want to know how we (and our damaged kin) are, and that they wouldn't be caught in the presence of our afflicted loved ones if they could possibly avoid it.

Years ago, I lost my brother Jim to undiagnosed madness and suicide. My marriage to my wife, Honoree ,produced two beautiful, musically gifted, and outgoing sons. Our younger, Kevin, bound for glory as a guitarist, took his life in our basement after enduring schizoaffective disorder for three years.[1][2] Our surviving son, Dean, lives on with us, stricken with a milder psychosis a few years afterward.

So, I asked myself: a book of letters written by mothers, sisters, and caregivers to insane people—with "Hope" in its title? What's the scam going on here?

I scam-skimmed rapidly through the pages of *Hope for Troubled Minds* on that first read-through: on full alert, prepared to be Offended, cranking up my arm to fling Tony Roberts's manuscript across the room.

But I didn't do the fling. In baseball lingo, I balked. It turned out to be one of the more fortunate balks in my life.

More on that, but first a little bit about Tony Roberts.

Tony himself resides in the Sub-Nation. He showed symptoms of bipolar disorder at the unusually early age of 13. He persevered for several years, playing varsity basketball in his home state of Indiana. He entered the state's Hanover College in 1982 as a kind of post-hippie and excelled in his studies.

Yet the affliction would not relax its grip on him. (It never does on its own.) He stumbled down the all-too-common rabbit hole of "self-medication," taking refuge in what he has described as a life of "sex, drugs, and more folk rock than roll." He maintained what he called a "love-hate relationship" with the Presbyterian church and eventually discovered that many people in his extended family bore various diagnoses of SMI.

Tony's bipolar disorder was confirmed by diagnosis in 1995, when he was 30. Confirmed, but not cured: He went through psychotic episodes, spent time in psychiatric hospitals, saw his marriage rocked, and, in 2009, was confirmed for mental health disability.

Yet Tony Roberts never surrendered to the worst of the worst. His unstinting willpower, buoyed by a commitment to antipsychotic medication and the patient love of his wife, eventually did their stabilizing work. Tony now is a practicing mental health minister and serves as Chief Shepherd for Delight in Disorder Ministries. He has written two books. This is his third.

And on second reading, I found this book worthy. More than worthy; it deserves an honored place on the shelves alongside the growing literature of mental illness, those who suffer it, and those who witness it.

Those passages in *Hope for Troubled Minds* that made me wince on first reading are part of a context—a necessary context. The context is humanization and love.

There is no shortage of discussion about "the mentally ill" these days. "The mentally ill" serve as convenient scapegoats for some of our worst societal problems. Our epidemic of gun violence, for instance: There's no need to sweep military-style assault rifles off the streets and out of homes. Just "do a better job with mental health" and things will be fine. (That is an actual quotation from a governor whose state had just witnessed a school massacre, and who, the previous month, had slashed more than $200 million from his state's mental healthcare budget.)

This particular governor does not know and/or does not care, by the way, that only about 25 percent of mass shootings in America are carried out by insane shooters.[3] Or that on the day of any such shooting in 2020, an average of 134 other people died from firearm injuries."[4] Or that nearly half of people who die by suicide had a known mental health condition: The mentally ill are a far greater danger to themselves than to others.[5]

Most Americans are as clueless as the governor on these matters. They are clueless for several reasons. Among the most powerful, a psychiatrist once told me, is primal fear. "[It is] the origin of all the misinformation, the projections, the denial, the blaming of the victims or the patient, the lack of empathy toward sufferers, treating adolescents as criminals . . . Human beings are terrified of this disease, and they try to deny it out of existence."[6]

It is for this very reason that *Hope for Troubled Minds* is not merely a worthy book, but an essential one.

You will indeed find the stories of raw pain and heartbreak that I overlooked on my grumpy first read-through. The agony in these messages can be unbearable, and it amounts to an indictment of the shamefully broken system of American healthcare.

But the element of hope—Hope—has its place too. Hope is what pulls apart the collective, abstracted phrase, "the mentally ill," and re-shapes it into individuals: distinctive individuals, each with a distinct core personality, each with a distinctive story to tell—a story that insists upon the dignity and the integrity of each subject of each message. "Hope" insists that we never, ever confuse or conflate the affliction with the soul of the victim. "Hope" insists upon reclamation and reform.

Read this book and join the cause.

---

[1] The scarcity of men's voices—in this collection, yet also in support and activist groups—is a phenomenon that merits further attention.
[2] Schizophrenia, schizoaffective disorder, bipolar disorder, and a few others are variants of the same root cause: genetically flawed brain cells that can become prodromal (actively developing into psychosis) when such external factors as traumas, stress, or grief overwhelm the carrier.
[3] https://www.aamc.org/news-insights/it-s-tempting-say-gun-violence-about-mental-illness-truth-much-more-complex
[4] Ibid.
[5]https://www.betterhealth.vic.gov.au/health/conditionsandtreatments/mental-illness-and-violence
[6] From a conversation with the psychiatrist John Edwards.

Ron Powers *is a Pulitzer-prize winning journalist (The Chicago Sun-Times) and an Emmy-winning television commentator (CBS News Sunday Morning). His most recent book is* No One Cares About Crazy People: My Family and the Heartbreak of Mental Illness in America.

Preface

Micah Pearson

You know most writers say that endings are the most difficult to write, but I find that I often struggle with the beginnings. So, of course, I'm the one who gets invited to write the preface to the journey we, the readers of this book, are about to partake in together. Fortunately, I've spent a little more than the last decade working with and advocating for those living with mental health conditions. More than that, I've lived with a few of those very same conditions my entire life. I intimately know the highs, lows, and manifest phantasms of bipolar disorder; the tension and fear of post-traumatic stress; and a few other diagnoses besides.

As much as I wouldn't trade my brain and the myriad of things it provides, it can be so
> very
>> exhausting.

After years of alcoholism, bouncing in and out of both employment and treatment, including in-patient hospitalizations, I ended up where far too many of us living with these conditions go: the de-facto mental health hospital also known as the county jail. Those last bits mostly happened over the course of a single year. By every estimate, from doctors to social workers, law enforcement, friends and family, and hell—even myself—at the rate I was going, I had a life expectancy of maybe two months. At most. That was 12 years ago.

Why did I spend 229 of my 1,000 allotted words telling you all this? Because one of the main reasons I'm alive today is the fact that my family and those closest to me dug deep and lifted me out of the morass I almost buried myself in. Not only that, they continued to do so as I repeatedly tried to claw my way back there. That's the "why" behind the work I do, the underlying drive behind the mission to advocate for others who live with struggles similar to my own. That is the only way I can express the limitless love and gratitude I have for the legion who cared for me when I needed it most. Even as a speaker or writer of books and countless essays and articles in journals and publications, I still can't find the right words.

Trust me, it's not for the lack of trying either. I've spent most of my life in love with words and language. So much so that in my junior year of high school, I got kicked out of English class after first hearing the word "onomatopoeia." For those not aware, onomatopoeia are words that sound like their meaning. Things like "bang," "whoosh," or "pow." I love that there's a word for that. There are words for everything. Like "defenestration," or the act of throwing someone out of a window.

Come to think of it, that one's a bit disturbing. Back to onomatopoeia.

I was kicked out of class because after I heard the word, I couldn't stop repeating it over and over. I even got to the point of making it into a little song: "Onomatopoeia! Onomatopoeia! Onomatopoeia! Onomatopoeia with the cheese on top!"

Over and over again it went, irritating everyone in the room, teacher and classmates alike. But I thought it was funny, so I just kept going. In actuality, I couldn't stop myself. Someone knocked a book off their desk and I shouted "Bam! That's an onomatopedism!" Didn't even use the word correctly. I just loved it so much.

I was 15.

It wouldn't be until I was diagnosed with bipolar disorder when I was 22 that we would realize that it was a mania-induced compulsion.

That said, I've always had a passion for words and language, mental health conditions or no. Words are strength and power. Because communication breaks down walls more effectively than any hammer. Words change hearts and minds. This is the definition of advocacy.

Over the years, I stopped referring to my conditions as "illnesses." You'll note that I've never called them that so far. This was a personal and conscious choice. I manage them day to day, and when I get ill, then I'm ill and have an illness. But I'm not sick all the time, so why look at it that way? Why encourage others to look at me that way? So I stopped, stopped allowing others, and my world changed. The attitude in the rooms changed, both towards me and those for whom I was advocating.

That, my friends, is the power of language.

Yet with all that passion and love for words and language, I still struggle to find the right way to express my gratitude to those who keep rising to the call.

That's what this book is about. What follows are letters of those who have risen to that challenge and put pen to paper, or fingertips to keyboards, rather. It is a compilation of that same love and gratitude those of us often struggle to express. While living with these conditions is frequently exhausting, yet we get up every morning and live our lives to the fullest. We come in all shapes, sizes, and colors, each walking our own path with pride. Some walk in faith, while others like myself who do not engage in a spiritual tradition walk without. But we all share the common bond of lived experience and the strength that it brings.

Yet I know, as strong as we are, we can look around us and see our families of both origin and choice, shouldering the weight with us.

Micah Pearson *(he/him) is Founder and CEO of Inside Out (http://ioadvocacy.com) and the Second VP NAMI Board of Directors. Among other things, Micah Pearson has served on a number of boards,* *including the New Mexico Governor's Behavioral Health Council in 2021. He has testified in front of legislatures to address and change the systems that deny care, perpetuate stigma, and criminalize mental health. He has been a guest speaker and/or published in journals for the American Psychiatric Association, Treatment Advocacy Center, and NAMI.*

Part One: Letters

Chapter 1. To the Children

The Great Thief

Randye Kaye

Dear Ben,

Life has not turned out to be what any of us imagined, hoped for you, when you were a little boy.

You: so bright, so sweet, so enthusiastic, so loving.
So many friends, so many talents. The future, so promising.

And then came schizophrenia. The great thief.

Oh, the symptoms presented in many forms before we—or at least I—understood what had happened.

As is so common with this illness, you don't think you have it. You fight that thought with all the stubbornness you've shown since birth, Taurus baby.

But I know.

I know that, but for this brain condition, you might be independent, working steadily, maybe married and parenting—whatever it is you wanted for yourself when you dreamed as a child.

What we all wanted for you.

Your sister's children might have cousins. You might buy me flowers on my birthday. You might meet old friends from high school or college for dinner and drinks.

But no. The great thief came along.

So, instead—hospitalizations; a roulette wheel of medications you still don't think you need; and a succession of lost jobs, lost friends, lost opportunities. Lost milestones.

And yet you try. You try your best to shine—most of the time.
One of the things I love about you is your optimism when a new chance comes along. Maybe it isn't always realistic, and maybe it doesn't always work out, but you still try.

There was a decade of some success, when you were on different medications and more pieces of you fell into place. You earned almost 60 college credits. You succeeded as a restaurant server, once you found the right fit. You leased your own car. You paid your own bills.

You felt proud of your life—despite still living at home with your parents.

But then. But then.

There is always something.

Covid causing the restaurant crash. No job.

Marijuana. Escape with consequences.

More success at spitting out your medications, despite our supervision.

And, there you were, back at square one: involuntary commitment for psychiatric reasons. Bankruptcy. Move to a group home again.

I have lost you a thousand times—and like a favorite beaded bracelet that breaks and scatters all over the floor, I've found pieces of you over and over again, but never the complete set.

Sometimes I can restring the bracelet, though it never looks quite right. Something is always missing.

What's missing is your clarity, your joy. What's missing is your hope. What's missing is your future.

My love for you is so deep that, like many mothers, I can forget how firmly entrenched it is into my heart, my very being. When you are doing okay, I rejoice. When you fall, I try not to worry, try to let go.

This has happened before. It's your life. It is what it is.

But, oh, my heart. My heart sobs. It weeps for you.

But you seldom complain. You don't exactly embrace with enthusiasm, but you keep going.

Last year you got yourself a job once again—minimum wage this time, but you didn't complain.

You showed up on time, you did the work, you learned new skills.

But your body, now on a different, older medication that causes tremors, wasn't cooperating.

Your employer thought something was wrong with your work ethic, not your health.

He had no idea you have schizophrenia. How could he, when you never would tell him?

You don't believe it yourself.

And, even if you did—would you be hired if they knew? The stigma is very, very real.

So. Hours reduced, then down to zero. Not fired, exactly; just kind of squeezed out. Again.

And that was so hard for you. You had been so hopeful, so happy to have a place to be, and a job to do—even when duties were reduced to unloading the truck. It still was a job. It still looked like a life.

And yet—you still try your best.

Despite all the disappointment you might feel when you look back at your life so far, you still try. You still hope, when the stars are aligned just right.

You will try again.

Meanwhile, you can be an uncle. When you are with the family, you pull it together to play with your nieces and nephew. They adore you.

You put on a brave face.

But, inside . . . inside. What do you feel?

I understand why you might want to escape with marijuana, why you—in your words—"think it'll make me feel good when I don't feel good—but it doesn't. And I still think it will work the next time."

And you try to stay clean—for the sake of seeing your family.

You want to work, you want to have purpose, you want a future.

But the great thief, schizophrenia, won't even let you know that it is not your fault. Given the choice—despite the evidence the illness won't let you see—you would stop taking your medication, you would smoke more weed, you would rely on some magical fairy tale to make your life work somehow.

I'm so grateful that, for the sake of being able to be with the family, you agree to stay clean and sober and stay on meds. At least this week.

I'll take it.

It's the best we can do for now and when I see your nieces and nephew light up to see you, run into your arms, and lead you to your old room to play Mario, my heart sings as best it can.

Every day that we get to make some new good memories to add to what we have, I am grateful.

As I am grateful for your sweet, loving nature. You are doing your best.

I can only hope that life will give you more of what you deserve.

Love,
Mom

Randye Kaye *is the author of* Ben Behind His Voices: One Family's Journey From the Chaos of Schizophrenia to Hope *(Rowman &* Littlefield, 2011), and Happier Made Simple: Choose Your Words, Change Your Life *(Front Porch Press, 2022). She's also an actor, voice talent, radio broadcaster, audiobook narrator, teacher, and speaker. She co-hosts several podcasts, including Schizophrenia: 3 Moms in the Trenches. She lives with her husband in Connecticut, and her children and grandkids live close by. Her dining room and living room are full of toys.*

The Power of Three

Julia Ehret

My dearest adult daughters, two years ago none of us were in contact with one another. We didn't know then that a miracle was about to happen. Through many trials and tribulations, we each found our way back to one another. And we agreed to support each other for the rest of our lives. Thank you, daughters, for putting your trust in me. Thank you for being grateful for your medication. Thank you for loving our new home which we have made together. Thank you for loving me. We are the power of three.

Love,
Mom

Julia Ehret writes, *"Had my fully disabled SMI adult daughter been diagnosed properly by age 18, then she'd be an allowable beneficiary to my SS retirement. She is 34 now and living with me again since last July, along with her 32-year-old, partially disabled SMI sister. We recently moved from California to Illinois and successfully averted poverty and homelessness."*

I Love You More Than You Will Ever Know

Angie Collier

Dear Jacob,

I loved you from the start. Your bright red hair, chubby cheeks, and the last of my three children. Your brother and sister adored you—holding you, telling you stories, reading to you. You loved lining your Hot Wheels from your bedroom to the living room. You quickly learned to read and you have an incredible vocabulary.

At eight you started hearing voices. We took you to a doctor who put you on medicine, but your depression plunged. In middle school, you started drugs to self-medicate and later alcohol. At 15, you were diagnosed with Schizoaffective Disorder.

The voices, paranoia, seeing things, and violence have been too much to endure, but my love for you has not stopped. You hit the walls causing holes and break my dishes, but then you apologize and my heart melts. You can dance and tell jokes that draw me in. I love to hear you telling me the latest thing you heard in a movie or documentary. I love you more than you will ever know.

I cry for your life being taken away by this terrible disease. At 26, we can't get you stabilized because of your drug use. When you are unstable, we are afraid. I want so much for you. I pray that when you are stable, you will do what you need to do to remain stable.

You are such an important part of my life.

Love you forever,
Mom

Angie Collier *is a teacher and NAMI volunteer. She quit her full-time job in order to be more available to her son. She currently works as a reading specialist online.*

To My Beautiful Son Dillon

Amy Swartz Kerr

Happy Birthday to my beautiful son Dillon. How can I express in words the love I have for you? To me you are a warrior who faces insurmountable battles every day, just to survive. Your courage and bravery bring me to tears. If I could only take this heavy yoke and wear it for you, I would. To give you a life of peace, there is no price I would not pay. Your love for family is just one of your beautiful qualities to admire. You're the type of person that considers it an honor to hold the door for the elderly, women, children, and especially your mom. You appreciate and love animals and nature, and especially your beloved dog "Duke," who's been blue ever since you left.

Today I only get to see you for an hour. They won't allow me to shower you with gifts or let me cook you your favorite meal or bake you your favorite chocolate peanut butter cake. But I'm thankful you're with us today, heading down a road of healing. I'm thankful that there are so many people who are still keeping you in their thoughts and prayers, and who want nothing but the best for you.

You are so loved, my sweet son. I pray you feel this support, and it continues to give you courage to fight this battle all the days of your life. With all my love, Happy 27th birthday, to the apple of my eye. I am so blessed to have you as my son.

Dear Bobby

Ann Corcoran

Dear Bobby,

One of my greatest accomplishments in life was becoming your mother. I had hopes and dreams for the man you would become. Your intelligence, compassion, and determination in everything you did brought me a great sense of pride. Bipolar disorder no doubt changed the way I see the world and what I now want for you, my loving son.

This brain illness at times has made you say and do things uncharacteristic of the person that I know is deep inside of you. It is an illness that has caused much turmoil for you. For this, I am deeply sorry and only wish that as your mother I could take the pain away. Despite great suffering, despair, and heartbreak, bipolar disorder has taught me so much.

It has taught me that we live in a world where those with serious brain disorders are discriminated against. We live in a society that accepts homelessness and incarceration rather than providing treatment to those who are too sick to ask for it. I have been motivated by these injustices to turn my pain into actionable change, to make things right for those afflicted with illnesses that are no fault of their own. I have learned how to be the voice for the 22 million people that live with serious brain disorders.

Your illness has helped me to become a more compassionate and nonjudgmental person. I no longer take anything for granted and appreciate the small things in life—a sunny day, the sounds of waves crashing, or a moment that makes me laugh. A day without chaos is truly a blessing.

I have met some wonderful and truly exceptional people in my journey as a mother who has experienced the unthinkable—having a child diagnosed with a serious brain disorder. These are friendships like no other. Though I have never met any of these friends in person, I hold each and every one close in my heart as they truly understand the struggles we go through. We recognize each other's trials and tribulations and are there to support one another. We are all fighting to make this a better world for those that live with these debilitating illnesses. These friends and their advocacy work provides me hope—hope that we will become a more compassionate and just world, and the suffering will end for those that live with serious brain disorders and their families.

I still have hopes and dreams for you, my loving son. I hope that you find stability. I hope that you can forgive me when I thought I was doing the right thing in getting you help and it made your life harder. I hope that you find happiness. I hope that you find the healthiest version of yourself. I hope that you find love. I hope that you find purpose. I hope that you find the life that you are happy with.

Despite all that we have been through, I have never been more proud of you. I am proud of the strength you exhibit in living with bipolar disorder—this is no easy feat. I am proud of you in trying to navigate a world that is so unjust to people that live with these illnesses. I am proud of you for the level of compassion you continue to show to others. I am proud of you for never giving up on yourself. I am proud of you for recognizing when you are struggling and need time for self-care. I am proud of you for being able to recognize your triggers. I am proud of you for wanting to pursue your dreams. But most of all, I am proud to be your mother and this will never change. I love you!

Love,
Mom

Ann Corcoran, *RN, MSN, is a nurse consultant, advocate/activist. She is passionate about improving the lives of those that live with mental illness and serious brain disorders.*

Dear Calvin
Jerri Clark

Dear Calvin,

I wish you were still here to know how much your life matters to me and to others who will benefit from the beautiful gifts you brought to this Earth. You were my wonder boy—smart beyond belief and full of enthusiasm. I loved to watch you swim, surf, snowboard, and reveal your amazing mind in speech and debate tournaments. When you called someone a friend, you meant it and remained loyal. You said "I love you" with your soft, kind eyes.

The change in your gaze was one of the ways I first knew something was wrong. When psychosis pulled you deep, something went missing behind your eyes. Your stare was fierce, yet empty. When your brilliance started to dim, my messy grief got mixed with deep confusion. You were you, but not you. You were still here, but not present. No one understood my mourning because you weren't gone, although to me it felt that way. They better understood what to do after you actually died. Then they brought flowers and soup and sat down to listen. I wish more people had done that all along. I felt so alone, always wishing for you as I had imagined you into the future.

During your journey through psychosis, which was mixed with mania and your rage-filled depression, you kept trying to come back. There were moments when recovery was almost possible, when we clung to one another, you and me. But the deck was stacked against you. Most of the "help" made you get dangerously unwell first and then cut away before you made significant progress. When you slipped, your eyes became holes. You lost track of who you and I were to each other. You could not see that the threat was inside your own mind. Instead, you lashed out at me. I was terrified for both of us.

When your brilliant mind betrayed you, it was only the beginning of the betrayals. Hospitals locked you up until they turned you out with nothing. Overworked providers said crime and jail were a better route to services. The healthcare system's shell game left you with bigger losses each time it spit you out.

You always came back to us, but professionals prioritized your autonomy over your life and never helped us help you. After your college career ended in crisis at age 19, you lost almost all of your friends and opportunities. Your mental illness was so severe and so poorly cared for that you checked every box on the list of brutal outcomes in less than four years: incarceration, homelessness, forced hospitalizations, isolation and restraint, suicide attempts.

Your final act ended your life, but your story isn't over. I'm going to make sure your pain continues to matter as I advocate fiercely for the "system" to learn from its mistakes and change. My advocacy work is in your honor, my son. We are working to make sure people get the treatment they need and stop being punished for becoming ill.

I know you are near because of the owls. Their eyes have a story to tell, and I listen with my heart when an owl appears. I hope you are in a realm where you know how important you still are.

"How wonderful it is that nobody need wait a single moment before starting to improve the world." Anne Frank said that. Her life mattered too. Like you, she deserved so much more. We can do better, and we will. Thank you for showing us the work that needs to be done.

Love,
Mom

Jerri Clark *is a grandma, a surfer, and a survivor who lost a son to SMI. She believes in speaking truth to power. She started Mothers of the Mentally Ill (MOMI) and supports families as part of her job at Treatment Advocacy Center.*

Dear KyLee
Charla Collins

Dear KyLee,

When I was 17 years old, I enlisted in the Air Force. I had known at a very young age that I wanted a life devoted to the service of others. I was the oldest of four and already knew what sacrifice was—or at least I thought I did. I enjoyed my time in the Air Force and my short stint in law enforcement but chose a different path because I felt I was too optimistic, and in law enforcement, you were always waiting for someone to make a mistake.

Instead, I chose to go to college and work as a paralegal. Divorced young, I learned sacrifice as a parent. I was a single parent for 16 years. Sometimes I worked two jobs and went to college full-time. I had aspirations of going to law school and making a real impact in the world. Then, two months shy of my bachelor's degree, I received the call no parent ever wants to receive. My beautiful 11-year-old daughter was struck by a car while riding her bicycle on the sidewalk. She wasn't wearing her helmet and suffered a traumatic brain injury.

For the next several years, every spare moment was spent trying to get KyLee back together again. Initially, physical therapy for the displaced hips. Then there was vision therapy for the loss of tracking, remedial schooling for the five years of math and reading that had been lost, but the one therapy that has never seen an end was psychological—every therapy known to man from cognitive behavioral to light therapy for PTSD.

Just when it seemed like things were going to stabilize, the hospitalizations began. The first was for cutting or self-harm, the next for an eating disorder, both of which I would prefer over any of the stints in rehabilitation for drug use. Multiple treatment centers of various kinds. More overdoses than either of us can count. Then the birth of the oldest grandson—two more would follow. I thought for sure you would stay sober, but I was wrong. The next big blow was schizoaffective disorder, a diagnosis you received at just 25 years old. Seven missing posters later, I feel like I may never get my KyLee back again.

Dear KyLee, I want you to know exactly how much I love you. You have been so special, so precious to me since the moment you opened your eyes. I knew my life would never be the same. I prayed, oh how I prayed for you. I wanted so badly to have a little girl. My mom would tell me when I was a teenager, "Charla, I hope you have a daughter just like you," and KyLee, you did not disappoint. I couldn't have been prouder.

We were inseparable for almost 12 years. We went on so many adventures from train rides to SeaWorld to Disneyland at Christmas. Then one trauma after another struck. Slowly my little girl was almost unrecognizable. However, mama can always see you, the real you. I am so sorry that the last few years have really taken a toll on our relationship.

Please know that if I would have had any indication of the abuse you were enduring behind closed doors with your boyfriend, I would have definitely intervened. It is the straw that broke the camel's back, and it is not your fault.

I know that you do not care for the medication that you are required to take, but it is the only way a glimpse of you can still be here. All three boys miss you terribly and argue over whose house is going to be bigger to make room for mama to leave the hospital and come live with them.

One of the harder conversations I had with your youngest is, why is mommy not getting better? My reply was, "Honey, I do not know the answer, but someday when I go to heaven, I am going to ask God." I refuse to give up hope, although I admittedly experience some days when it is easier to see than others.

If I could really have you hear one thing it would be this—I would gladly take your place. If there was a way to trade places with you, I would. You see, I love you that much. I want nothing more than for you to experience the joy that I have…to see your boys grow up and to be part of their life. To live a life where you're not trying to be invisible and avoid the world.

Honey, the world is an amazing place. Think about some of the adventures we went on when you were younger. I would love for you to have those same experiences with your boys. They would do anything to see you again. They are some of the most forgiving people you will ever know. They are so young and would do anything to hang on to, hold, and love on their mama. It is so precious, just like you. With my last breath I will pray for you. I pray for you to come back to us. I pray for a happy, healthy, and loving life. I pray someday you will love yourself as much as we love you. I pray for healing. I also pray that you will see yourself as the beautiful woman you are and the amazing mother you can be.

You Are Loved
Deacon Carter Hawley

Dear Jessie,

When you first came to live with us, you were a frightened, abandoned four-year-old. You were in a few foster homes before you came to live with us permanently. When we'd tuck you in, we'd remind you of three things. You are loved. You are safe. You are not going anywhere. This was your forever home, and you were forever loved.

Sometime during high school, you got sick. We didn't know at first, and I bet you didn't either. It was frightening for us, and if it was scary for us, I'm sure it was scarier for you. You seemed to get further and further away from us, and yet we loved you.

Eventually, you ended up with a pretty serious brain disorder diagnosis that provided answers, but no solutions. It was one of the few times I saw your dad cry. You'd spend time in hospitals and jail, and we were glad—because we knew where you were and you were safe.

We worked hard to keep track of you—tracking you down at a bus station in East L.A. when you ran away, and twice again in Oregon. We tracked you down in jail, despite your attempts to hide from us, and we met you when you were released. We will always try to find you.

As we've told you, you have an indomitable spirit—you cannot be crushed, and you have been an inspiration to us, as this disease takes its toll. We are with you all the way and will be with you always. You are loved. You are safe. You are not going anywhere.

Love,
Mom & Dad

Carter Hawley writes, *"As the mother of an adult child with a severe brain disorder, I know firsthand the importance of advocacy for troubled minds. My daughter is still my cherished daughter, and it's easy to forget that everyone with a severe brain disorder has been cherished by someone."*

My Beloved Son

Audrey Auernheimer

My beloved son,

Wow! What a journey it has been for the past 31-plus years.

I remember clearly the day you were born. You took your time making an entry and seemed a bit reluctant to leave your safe, warm environment. After the third visit to the hospital with "false" labor, I was again told to go home and wait a while longer. I groaned. After a month suffering from gestational diabetes and chronic indigestion, I was feeling every minute of my 40 years. Also, I was growing impatient, waiting to meet that tiny infant who had tumbled around happily inside me for the past few months.

After being told to go home and wait, I announced to any medical professional within hearing that I was not leaving that hospital without my baby in my arms! Much to my relief, they agreed to keep me overnight. A nurse brought medication to help me sleep, and I dozed for a short time, only to be awakened by hard cramping and back pain. It was time. Finally!

Two and a half hours later, you made your way into the world with a loud cry of triumph! As I held you in my arms for the first time, I examined your toes and tiny fingers and watched you smile at me. You were such a beautiful, perfect baby boy! My feelings of love for you were almost overwhelming, sweeping me away to a height of joy only a mother can feel toward her newborn.

I remember watching your dad's face light up as he gazed at you with such wondrous joy on his face. After leaving the hospital he went to a friend's house and talked for hours about your miraculous birth. He talked about the overflowing love he felt when he first saw you, and how humbling it was to realize God had answered his prayer for a son. He talked about his feelings of inadequacy at the thought of parenting this tiny child that was now his responsibility. Our friend and her husband described it as "catching the bubble" of joy.

Oh, my dear son! Never question your beginnings. I cannot imagine any child entering this world who was more loved, wanted, and cherished by his parents than you were and are.

The first time your half-sister Candace met you at eight years old, she squealed with delight. The two of you shared a close sibling bond from the beginning. That bond was strengthened later in life when she came to live with us and the two of you attended the same Christian school, you in kindergarten, her in middle school. Candace had lots of friends, and you quickly became known as "Candace's little brother," a title you happily accepted. At elementary school, you loved helping me in the kitchen and I remember how you loved spicy foods. You sprinkled red pepper on almost everything! Those are happy memories.

A couple of weeks ago, your dad and I made the five-hour trip to visit you in another state. A couple of months earlier you had left our warm, comfortable home to live in a storage shed—a sturdy, but rather squalid storage shed in a large city, with no utilities and no plumbing. I didn't understand. Winter was on its way. How would you keep out the cold?

Our lives have changed so drastically within the past 16 years. What happened to change your life so drastically? How did we, as a caring, stable family, get to this place?

Shortly after your medical diagnosis of Psychosis NOS (Not Otherwise Specified) at age 14, a series of multiple hospitalizations began, followed by repeated drug treatments, juvenile detention lock-up, therapy, and frustratingly little effective treatment for your illness. Your Dad and I didn't always understand how much of your behavior was related to illness symptoms. I apologize for our anger during this difficult time.

When you were 17, we received the news that your sister had taken her life. The news hit you hard. Your beautiful sister, confidante, and best friend was gone, and you wrongly blamed yourself. We watched your life quickly spin out of control. A year or so later, addiction- and illness-related criminal charges led to you serving six years in prison. As a result of a pre-sentencing evaluation, your diagnosis was changed to Schizoaffective Disorder/Bipolar type.

We are proud of you achieving your GED while incarcerated. Upon release from prison, you remained drug free, took the initiative to get a full-time job, and aced several college classes. Your courage, amazing resourcefulness, and determination to survive while battling demons in your head is nothing short of awe-inspiring! Some traits I admire in you are your intelligence, quick wit, heart of compassion, and generosity. These have never changed.

I am proud of you, son.

I am Mom. My love has never wavered from that overwhelming joy I felt the first time I saw your face. The love your dad has for you now is the same as it was then. That will not change. You are precious to us. We will never give up on you, son. With faith, you will have everything necessary to recover from your illness and succeed in life.

As an adult, where and how you live your life is your choice. Our prayer is that we can establish some sort of communication with you. These long trips become difficult, as we age.

Life is teaching me to let go, let God. It brings peace knowing that no matter how far away you are from me, you can never move too far away from your God, Protector, Provider, and Healer. God loves you even more than I am capable of.

We will always be here for you. Meanwhile, we are entrusting you to our merciful Father's care.

Love forever and always,
Mom

Audrey Auernheimer writes, *"For 11 years, I was an active advocate for family members and for those suffering Serious Mental Illness in central Kansas. My husband and I also facilitated a NAMI (National Alliance of Mental Illness) support group, and taught Family to Family education classes for family members of the mentally ill. My husband and I have retired to the state of Oklahoma, nearer to family. I continue to advocate for change in the laws regarding SMI by way of online advocacy groups."*

Dear Tariq

Diane Rabinowitz

Dear Tariq,

I want to tell you how much I love you, and how happy I am that you are finally in a care situation where you have recovered much of yourself. In some ways you are doing better than you ever have, even before you got sick. You are reading now, you are communicating so well now about your activities, your thoughts, your feelings. You are not afraid of your feelings; you are caring for yourself in ways that I've never seen before. It is truly a miracle and a wonder of prayers answered, sufferings endured.

I remember when I got that first call from the police telling me that you were in trouble, and I needed to get home "now." They had you in a squad car. They asked me if I had seen the wounds on your arms and legs. I had only seen one of the wounds the previous day; I had asked you about it and you said it was nothing, you just fell skateboarding. It turned out that you had large burns on your arms and your legs, and we had to take you to a burn specialist for him to make sure they did not get infected.

Days later, you insisted on going to your friend Raymond's house, after his mother told you were not welcome there. I chased after you and had to call the police. I did not and could not understand your behavior, but I felt it was dangerous. I had no way to deal with the trauma we were both experiencing other than to ask for help from those who were supposed to defend and protect us—the police. They showed up with a large fire engine, an emergency vehicle, and a couple of police cars. You were sitting on the curb. One of the fire men engaged you in conversation and I heard you tell him you burned yourself. When they finally got you in the ambulance, they took your blood pressure. It was off the chart. You were so anxious. I was so scared.

They took you to the hospital, and you were there for a month. Your dad and I drove the 35 miles and sat in traffic both ways and that doubled the travel time. Each visit was more suffering. You were very fragile.

Meanwhile, I was learning about a level of suffering that I had never known before. I developed much deeper compassion and empathy for my students, so I was able to do my job better. But I still was afraid because I didn't know how to help you. We tried family therapy. We tried having you see a psychiatrist. We tried putting you in a day program, but they hospitalized you. You weren't getting better. Finally, I realized that my insurance company was not going to help me get the treatment you needed, so I turned to the county, where we had our first successful engagement with treatment.

I was so proud of you when, after a year of working with your case manager, your therapist, and psychiatrist, you were able to go to college. I was thrilled that even though math had become harder for you than it had been before, you worked hard, you joined a study group, you had a girlfriend, and you seemed happy. You were taking piano lessons and you were actually learning to read music and play with two hands! Practice was paying off! You were starting to be able to play pieces well.

But it was during that third semester that things started to go bad. I saw you during the Christmas break withdrawing and not feeling so well, and you wouldn't talk to me. I knew you were going out with friends, and I had a feeling you were starting to smoke pot again. But I didn't realize that even though you had registered for a couple of classes, you weren't going to those classes. Instead, you started hanging out with some people that were scary to me.

I became very alarmed. It was evident that you were no longer taking your medication. Since the agency "graduated you" from the Full Service Partnership, you were not getting the support you needed to work through your challenges. I became filled with dread. We started fighting because you were lying to me, and I felt you were putting me in danger with the people you were hanging out with. Each time I called for help from the PET team, you were able to behave in such a way that they didn't believe you needed to be hospitalized again. But I knew there was something seriously wrong and I was frustrated that no one would listen to me.

Finally, you told me you wanted to leave home and asked if I would write you a check from your college money. When you left with your belongings in a duffle bag, I felt dreadful. And when my house was robbed, I had a feeling it was you and your new friends.

For the next eight years it was homelessness, jail, failed treatment over and over again. I was actually relieved when you were in jail, because at least I knew where you were, I could visit you, and you weren't homeless. Yes, there were dangers to being in jail. But after the third or fourth time, they had started a mental health wing at the jail. You had a clinician to meet with, and they were giving you medication. I'm sure it wasn't ideal. But Dr. Weiss became a good friend to both of us, and believe me, he has helped us get this far. You have been conserved for three years now, and we have finally been able to get you into a treatment facility that has worked wonders.

I pray every day that the support you've gotten will continue so that you may continue to recover and have a safe, healthy, fulfilling life. My faith and my joy have deepened tremendously over these 12 years of suffering and struggle. I pray that you will find a faith that you can turn to, that sustains you. I am grateful for you, my son, my greatest gift in life.

Diane Rabinowitz *enjoys life in a small rural Sierra Foothills town in Northern California, daily serenaded by birds, goats, chickens, dogs, horses, and her opera-singing neighbor. She is active in the local NAMI* *affiliate, determinedly advocating for families and their loved ones. Her Nichiren Buddhist practice inspires her to fight for people with mental health challenges to get access to treatment and opportunities to live and thrive in safety and community.*

To My Miracle Child
Donna J. Erickson

It has not been easy since day one. Actually, before that. I had fertility problems that required tests, treatments, and lots of doctor visits.

What came so easily for others was an uphill struggle for me. I just wanted to have a baby. Jeff and I married young, worked hard, and saved up enough money for a down payment on a house. After we moved in, my biological urge to become a mother really kicked in. But my body was not cooperating.

Finally, after four long years, my dream came true. I was pregnant!

Love Letter to My Son

Dear Ryan,
I loved and wanted you so much, before you were even born. When you came into our lives, your father and I were over the moon and filled with happiness.

But it was hard to raise such a defiant child. Tantrums lasted longer than my friends' children's, and I felt helpless.

We were devastated to learn that you had bipolar disorder at age nine. Medication came soon after. I knew your life would not be easy, because my mother had the same diagnosis, and I saw her struggle my whole life.

After you graduated high school, I felt your pain when your friends went their separate ways, and you felt lost. By age 25, you decided to try going off your meds, after reading online about potential side effects. My heart broke every time we had to call 911, because it became impossible to live with so many manic-psychotic episodes.

You had delusions that convinced you I was a child molester and a black witch. It hurt when you said you didn't want contact with me, but I kept telling myself it was the illness talking, not the son that I knew and loved. Year after year, I was losing hope. It was hard to see you go through more than 20 hospitalizations and slip further and further away. I prayed every night for a miracle. I cried so much that it felt like no more tears were left, but the tears still flowed.

After eight years of psychotic hell, you finally came back to us. My sweet boy had returned!

I'm still waiting for the other shoe to drop. It's been almost three years of stability, but it's hard to let go of the worry. I see it as nothing short of a miracle that God brought you back to us. Our unconditional love for you continued no matter how hard things got. We stood by you when you needed court-ordered medications, during several other court hearings, during your year-long state hospitalization, and every day since.

You have done an amazing job, and I'm so proud of the progress you have made. You are fully onboard with your treatment, and it's wonderful to hear you encourage others to stay on their meds. Recently, we were told you have met all your goals at the group home, including regularly attending a day program, and the next step will be your own apartment with supportive services.

I'm excited to see you mature and face the next phase of your personal journey. As long as I am alive, I will continue to offer my loving support. When I am no longer on Earth, you can be sure I'll be watching over you, with a mother's special love.

Donna J. Erickson writes, *"I was a certified Family Support Group Leader for NAMI, attended NAMI's Family-to-Family intensive 12-week training course, and have been an advocate for my MI son for 30* *years. As the retired former owner of a writing/editing/publishing service, I have authored numerous articles and essays on the topic of Mental Illness."*

To Neil

Diana Dunham Preston

Hi Neil,

I visited you at the cemetery last week and left you some new flowers. Margaret was in from Kansas at the end of May, and I knew she had been there from the red, white, and blue plants and decorations she left for you, mom and dad. I had to get the candle holder repaired and replanted; the lawn mower must have "bumped" it. It's all good now.

Daniel is remodeling and selling your aunt Sondra's house, who you know has passed away. He is really tearing it up with the work there. Some days I get on his nerves—no surprise.

I am having bad bouts with depression and some anxiety. I have had this forever, so it's not your fault, but I do miss you as much now, or more, than before. It's been 20 years now and you would be 40. I often wonder what you'd be doing, your career, if you have a family, just stuff in my head.

I'm 75 and when I see new posts on "I miss my son," so many are new losses and parents hoping their pain will get better. It really does not. I think I miss you more now. This grief is a changing thing. I haven't been to mass since Todd's dad's funeral at St Mary's, where all of the family funerals have been. I live right next door to the church, so no good excuse for staying away. I have to get back, but I struggle with it. I still talk to God—He's got me and you with Him. I hope He understands my neglect.

I see some of your friends on Facebook, but I wish people would talk more to me about you. It hurts family, I know, and some of my friends have difficulty. If they only knew how much it would mean to me. I'm okay and get past it. My blessing is knowing you're okay like you told me you were right after you passed away. Margie heard it, too, at about the same time.

I don't do any suicide stuff at WVU anymore. Everyone I volunteered with is retired now. No one really knows what I'm talking about, but the Wellness Center is still there in our building, and they offer so much more for students, including suicide prevention.

I so hope you can see what is happening here and you hear when I talk to you. Maybe I am getting closer to seeing you again. I try not to get on your brother's nerves. I could not handle making another son sick. I feel guilty for a lot of my stuff, alcohol to medicate my mental illness and leaving you at times to spend time with you-know-who, which now is my most intense regret. I could have been home with you. You were such a gentle soul, kind and giving to others, and your humor could keep me laughing. People remember how smart you were in school. I have two very smart sons I am so grateful for.

I miss Florida a lot, but being closer to Daniel is good. The memories of you here as a youngster playing ball, UHS, WVU, pull at my heart when I drive by these places. Oh my God, I wish you were here, not in this town but somewhere here, sometimes. It was all in God's hands and my being back here, too. I love you and Daniel so much my heart is just full of love for you two. I think you know that and wish I had been a much better mother. I will let that regret stuff go. Daniel hates the guilt and regret, and he's right.

I have been prescribed oxygen starting tomorrow because I haven't exercised and walked enough. You were the master at working out! Covid, depression, and moving have kept me inside. I need a swimming pool here like we had in Florida. Swimming is my love. I will find a place soon.

I don't know if you have seen Patty or Ruthie or Sondra. I will know someday who we see when we leave here.

Love,
Mom

Diana Dunham Preston writes, *"I am Richard Neil Preston's mom. Neil passed away by suicide on September 30th, 2003, after struggling with major depressive disorder, anxiety, and/or bipolar brain disease."*

For My Cyber Gladiator Son

Anonymous

For my wonderful son . . .

I cherish all the memories of my handsome, brilliant, surprisingly athletic, accomplished young son who had so very many gifts and seemingly limitless possibilities.

In your late teen years, we started to see a change—things were not making sense, and something seemed off. You recognized it in yourself and, at first, you fought hard, trying everything you could think of to escape the coming darkness.

Despite our best efforts, eventually you slipped into the darkness that overcame you, and you lost the will to come back to reality. I continue to keep trying to fight to keep you safe from your thoughts.

Please know that I will always love you. Every day, I grieve and mourn the pain of your lost potential and the life you should have had that will never be. All I want is for you to feel happy, calm, and at peace and to remember how much I care and will always be there for you.

I love you with all my heart and soul forever.

On Any Given Day, the Mother of Four

Aurora Williams

On any given day, I am the mother of four.

Each child brings something to the table. But only one has made me who I am. He has called me to be a better person. His mental illness has tried to shatter our world, but we seem to have survived.

To you, my son, I am grateful for you wanting to survive. I am grateful that you are concerned for others. We seem to be in a life-warp right now where psychosis is winning, but you reach out and want to talk. I will lean into the good times and memories of you before psychosis sets in. I will lean into the memories of you painting and cooking. I think some of my favorite memories are of you with Boris and Nattie. Also your multi-level garden in the front yard. Skateboarding always.

Love always wins; kindness always wins; compassion lines the path to wellness; empathy allows me to share the journey. Mine is a mother's journey—a journey different from your own. If we are each here to learn things the Creator set before us, what are you to learn from this? What am I to learn?

You told me to be a voice for those who cannot find their own. You have called me to be better than I am. You have set the bar of expectations high. For all of this I am grateful. I wish only that I could spare you the pain and anguish of a brain that has betrayed you. But I will believe that love always wins; kindness always wins; compassion lines the path to wellness; empathy allows me to share the journey. And I will lean into my Creator, and pray:

Dear Lord, will you please protect this child? Will You please heal him and deliver him to be the person You created him to be? Will You please continue to cultivate gratitude for all things? Will You calm us when the world gets noisy? Will You remind him he is a child of Yours and therefore he can give the battle to You? He has already won.

To My First Child, My First Real Love

Christa Davis-Overton

My first child. My first real love. You're never alone in this world. Only as alone as you choose to be or the trials of this life make you seem to be. The day you were born, you were welcomed into this imperfect world with the perfect love of me and your grandma Sharon. The prayers of your great grandmothers poured down on you like the lights shining brightly in the delivery room, guiding you into the hands of the physician as I pushed you into this world, not knowing what the next day held but knowing the love I felt as I held you in my arms for the very first time. I was so young. You were so perfect and beautiful.

Nothing has changed, my daughter. Your beauty and perfection don't cease to exist just because your father didn't choose to experience and be grateful for it or the men in your life didn't respect and/or deserve it. It didn't change the day you lay on the hospital bed and looked into my eyes and said, "Mom, please don't leave me. I'm scared. It hurts right here," as you pointed at your heart and stared into my eyes with a darkness and emptiness that encapsulated me like a thick fog on a dark country road.

I held your head in my arms not knowing which way to go. I felt my knees wanting to collapse and fall to the ground. My eyes filled with tears like a steady rain rolling down my face. I couldn't wipe my tears because I was wiping yours, wanting to make you feel safe. It was as if I was in the labor and delivery room giving birth to you again. I wanted you safe and healthy. I just wanted you to be okay.

Nothing has changed, my daughter. I still want the same things for you. And you are still beautiful and perfect in this imperfect world. Your journey is just a little bit less perfect with mountains higher and valleys lower than most.

You have given this life so much of you. Yet it has given you so much less than you deserve. There are things from the past that still haunt you— things that I didn't even know. But wasn't I supposed to know everything? Maybe I was so busy trying to make everything right I didn't see what was wrong. Or maybe what was wrong was too much for you to share because it didn't fit into our happy equation, we—like this world—have been working on our whole lives.

There is no blame or shame here, just unconditional love. There is no stigma because nobody's life is perfect unless it's edited and filtered on a screen to make the world give likes and loves to people, they can't really see and don't really know. The truth is my daughter . . . my queen . . . you have been knocked down so many times. I've been there and seen it all. And it was not those things that we see coming or plan for or even imagine. You are my dancer, who lights up any stage she is on. You are a winner at everything you touch.

I know it doesn't feel like it over these past few years, but Nyla, Victoria . . . what princesses you brought into this world. No one could do that but you. God chose you to bring royalty and beauty on this earth because that's what you are. I don't know what it must feel like to have your thoughts and mind twisted, bringing fear and paranoia to every corner, seeing those who love you as enemies on a battlefield—just wanting to be free and in charge on this battlefield we call life or not being able to comprehend why your life doesn't look like others or why others have made it look so easy.

But what I do know is I feel your every pain, shed every tear, and carry a heavy sadness in my heart because you are part of my heart. You don't know how many times I've asked God to take that burden from you and give it to me because I've lived most of my life but you've got the rest of yours, and I only want the best for you. Sometimes I get angry with God, and I question: why you—why me? Are you paying for a sin of my past?

Always reasoning and reckoning for an answer, when the answer is God. He knows the beginning from the end. I know that He has His hands on you. It's the only respite I know on those days and nights when my beautiful child speaks to me like a stranger on the street in an anger and hatred that has me in disbelief.

I want to lash back, but then I look in your eyes and see a totally scared stranger looking at me. I want to love you to life but I can't.

I want you to know that no matter what you say or do, there is nothing that will ever change my love for you. It doesn't matter what others say or do. It's a battle you are fighting and although it feels like you think you are alone, think again, my child.

Together with the power and strength of God, you will make it. You will rise. It's just that you will be much stronger and wiser than most because you, my queen, are facing and fighting a battle most will never know or imagine. You're in the fight of your life and whether you like it or not, I'm right in the ring with you.

I always have been and always will be even when you don't see or believe it. I'm your mom, you are my daughter. Together with God we can beat this thing. I know it.

Love,
Mom

Christa Davis-Overton *is the mother of two, grandmother of two, and a 26-year pharmaceutical professional whose passion is writing and sharing joy with all who are looking. She is committed to mental health advocacy and outreach.*

Dear B

Donna M.

Dear B,

I know that I've told you this many times, but I feel that it is something that bears repeating. I have known you and loved you since before you were born. You are one of the loves of my life.

Your grandmother, who had 11 children, always used to say that children are a miracle and a gift from God. Well, you were my first miracle. I wasn't sure if I was ready for this miraculous gift; I didn't know if I was up to the task. As the mysteries of this amazing (and sometimes harsh) experience unfolded for me, the love I felt for you grew stronger by the day. Cliché, but true. Imagine the wonderment that washed over me as I watched my belly undulate with your movements and when I felt those little hands and feet through my skin! I really was in total awe.

Throughout your growing years, I saw that God had blessed me with a warm, sensitive, kind-hearted child. I saw how you bore physical pain with great courage, and how hurt feelings required a lot more strength...sometimes more than you could muster. This sensitivity wasn't just for yourself, but for others as well. I love how you loved your little sister. I love how you loved your friends. I love how you loved your family . . . I love the person you are.

As I think about you, a memory of how you responded to your grandmother arriving on the night of your seventh (?) birthday just popped into my thoughts. When we picked her up, after a long day of fun and party and gifts, you greeted her with, "Nanny, today is my birthday and now it is the best birthday ever because you're here!" Your first inclination was to make her feel loved and welcomed.

Do you remember your kindergarten teacher? I don't remember her name, but she called me one day to report on your behavior. Her school board supervisor had visited your class recently to see how the new program was being implemented. Not long after her visit, she had to be admitted to hospital. Your teacher told your class about it and had all of the students sign a get-well card for her friend. After circle time, all of the kids forgot about it and ran off to play. . . all but one. You showed up at the teacher's desk a little while later with a picture you'd made. "Here, this is for your friend." Such a simple, but sweet gesture from a five-year-old.

Life wasn't all rosy for you and your sister, but the closeness and friendship you shared as you were growing up got you both through a lot of struggles. You had each other's back. I recently found an old notebook that you were using for the "club" you formed when you were kids. Among the list of rules was "We will love each other forever." I smile at the thought of my two little ones declaring their mutual affection and dedication.

I remember one of your friends in elementary school telling his mom he was bored. I realized at that moment that I had never heard you complain about boredom. You were always busy with something, and generally laser-focused on anything you were doing. Your creativity came out in your childhood passions—building with Legos, exploring nature, learning about space, playing with your calculator and discovering math, drawing, or writing stories (sometimes with cartoon characters drawn right into the letters of the words)! Better yet, you could share those activities with your friends!

As you got older and expanded your horizons, you continued to fill your time with new experiences and knowledge, and new friendships. I wish I could remember how many times others complimented you—from your seventh-grade workshop teacher who mentioned how you had expanded on the class activity and how no one else had thought to do that before, to the youth group leader who told me how helpful and likable you are, to all of the random people we encountered who asked if you were my son, and then told me what a nice young man you are. They were all telling me something that I already know. You are an intelligent, creative, kind gentleman.

Like your dad, your sister, and your niece, you are one of the loves of my life. I thank God every day for you. I am so proud to be your mom.

Love,
Mom

Donna M. *has accompanied her son on the SMI roller coaster since he first showed symptoms more than 15 years ago. She wants others to know that people like her son are not their illness, and deserve compassion, understanding, and respectful treatments.*

He's Still in There

Gibby

He is still in there. From time to time, I get to see my sweet, loving son. We get a few words that remind me of the son he once was. Then the creature that has taken up residence in my son's brain realizes he is gone and comes for him. Then we are back in the land of conspiracy, and I know he is gone again. Let the worry begin again. Till the next time, my son. I'll be waiting.

Coming Home—Inner Calling

Heidi Franke

Editor's Note: warning—graphic details of a suicide attempt.

If you or someone you know is thinking about suicide, please call 988 for the 988 Suicide and Crisis Lifeline or text the word HOME or START to 741741 for the Crisis Text Line.

At age 21, my son came home. Had he not done so, he would be dead.

I pay tribute to his endurance.

I have an original painting by Aaron Jasinski that depicts a woman on the telephone. The background is a dark blue, her face at the top of the painting and the long black cord of a telephone drifting to the bottom and disappearing. The connection did not go through.

She keeps calling him. To find him. An inner calling. Where is he? How lost is he tonight? Will you please come home? I was that mom. I was trying to reach my son.

Spending year after year, months upon months, breath after breath trying to keep my youngest son alive and safe from his serious and persistent mental illness.
I cannot imagine his own distress while running away at such an early age. He was 15 when he stopped coming home at night. He was 16 when we admitted him to the State Hospital where they diagnosed him with bipolar 1—the same brain ailment my father had.

At 18, he was eligible for Social Security Disability and he wanted to try to live on his own. Sadly, it didn't last long—not for want of trying, but he just didn't have all the skills he needed as yet to be fully independent and make healthy decisions.

At 21, he came home and that saved his life. On a summer evening, unbeknownst to myself, my son left the streets to sleep on the porch swing in the backyard. He had purposely overdosed to stop the voices. It was early the next morning that I found him pacing along the perimeter of the yard like a dog might do trying to find a place to relieve himself. My son was relieving himself from both ends of his body for he had attempted suicide and his body was trying to rid itself of all that he ingested.

His skin color was a pale gray. As a nurse, I knew he was in deep trouble. He was incoherent and was drifting in and out of a conscious state and was unable to speak much at all.

He had stopped throwing up and stooling in the dirt and on the grass. He made odd statements that I tried to put together. I wasn't sure if he had the flu but finally, he told me that he had heard voices telling him to kill himself because they/we were after him. He hadn't wanted to, but his paranoia got the better of him. It was easier to stop the noise and voices in his brain by taking his life.

911 was called and the first responder was a senior police officer for the City Police Department. It wasn't all that obvious at first to the police officer what was happening to him. I was still collecting information from him that would make sense. He did not readily tell us that he had taken an overdose.

His vomiting ramped up again, which was good, for it meant he was getting rid of any drugs left inside his GI tract. The officer was patient. He pressed my son on what was going on. It was then he was able to tell us that he had taken Tylenol, aspirin, and his psychiatric meds that were in his backpack. Bottles and bottles.

He went to two different gas stations. At the first one, he felt that someone was watching him, so he went to another gas station, and he took all of these medications—the full bottles except for a few remaining aspirins. He had taken these in the evening before I found him. His auditory and visual hallucinations continued.

We called an ambulance not too long after the police officer arrived. I followed the ambulance up to the hospital emergency department and stayed with my son the entire time.

The doctors indicated that he had toxic levels of medication in his system and his liver was failing. They started a medication called NAC which helps the liver in an overdose event. They hooked him up to fluids. Warmed up his skinny body. He was in physical pain as well. They continued doing serial blood draws. He remained very sleepy and difficult to arouse. When he did start to come around, he started to sob. He just cried for so long and asked for me to help him to get the voices to stop.

He asked, "Why is this happening? Why is this happening? Why is this happening?" I told him I don't know, but you are safe now. I'm here. I cautiously held his hand because I did not know what his voices may have been telling him, but he was okay with me holding his hand. I called him by name and said, "My hand is real. You are safe now. I am your mom. We're getting you help. You will get better." He needed to hear those words.

The doctors watched his liver enzymes for improvement, and they continued to be elevated in spite of the medication. They were debating whether they were going to admit him to the ICU in case his liver started to shut down altogether.

In these critical moments, time doesn't stop, but it swirls, and it kinks itself, cutting like sharp razors. Even I became bewildered and remained in shock.

He became medically stable in four to five days. The medical team decided he was stable enough to have him admitted to the Neuropsychiatric hospital where he usually goes.

That hospital stay was the longest hospitalization for him—over 30 days. Once any street drugs were out of his system, they could try to determine if this suicide attempt was related to his bipolar or something else. His favorite psychiatrist had mentioned to us in a joint session that people with bipolar disorder have a high risk of suicide. He said this 13 times in 30 minutes. I'll never forget that meeting.

After two weeks in the hospital, he was still paranoid. He was afraid to come out of his room. He thought people were laughing at him. He felt people could read his mind. He thought they were poisoning his food, so he stopped eating. That was a big concern. The team decided to put Saran wrap over his food. They told him the Saran wrap had prevented anyone from tampering with his food. It was safe for him to eat again. This cleverness worked.

This was the admission that gave my youngest son the diagnosis of schizoaffective disorder along with his bipolar 1, PTSD, and anxiety. Our world changed and has never been the same since.

There are so many nightmarish stories we have lived through the years. He is now 27.

I write this tribute because I am so grateful that my son came home that night! I'm so grateful to my son for using what wise mind he had left to come home where he knew I would never abandon him. He knew I would accept him again and again and again no matter what.

He is alive because he came home. I am grateful to my dear son for doing so!

May your suffering be eased. May you live with peace and more joy. May you be safe and healthy. I love you. Mom. Your father, if he were here, would concur. He loved you very much. Ye who are weary, come home. Honestly. Tenderly.

Heidi Franke writes, *"By trade a registered nurse. A mother in love. My father had bipolar, and my son has a similar illness. I want generational trauma to be handled more effectively."*

Only Kindness Matters

Laura Pogliano

When I think about writing a letter to my deceased son, I pause. What would I say to him today, eight years after the police who were sent for a welfare check discovered him in his apartment three minutes from my home, seemingly "asleep" in bed? It's impossible to convey.

I have at best mixed feelings about his passing, keenly wanting him here, wishing we could take advantage of better treatment, to be able to assist his recovery with so many things I've learned since his passing. Surprisingly, sometimes instantly, I'm jealous of families who have children who are doing well, but also keenly not wanting him here to suffer the kind of lives so many with serious mental illnesses live. Would I ask him to stay so he could be arrested or imprisoned or shot at by police or wander the streets as a homeless person? Emphatically, no. No matter what I say to him in this letter, here are things that will never change. He suffered inordinately. And he is gone.

There are so many things I would say to Zaccaria: but most of all, I am sorry.

I'm sorry if I didn't help you in the ways you needed.

I'm sorry if my help was oppressive, if it made you feel less worthy or somehow less of a person. I only had fear to guide me, and doctors, who are not as focused on the person as they are on the illness. I had love to guide me, but it was mostly overridden by this primal fear and all it infused me with. What if he misses a dose of medication? What if he can't find his way home with his bus ticket? What if he gets taken advantage of because his capacity is compromised?

I tried so hard to engineer your life, thinking that better health was just around the corner and that I could force you to get well if I just tried harder. Eight years after your death, I can see that I was overbearing—a smother, not a mother. It's not what I wanted, and I'm sorry.

I'm sorry if my love was oppressive. If I smothered you when you needed release. If I bullied my way into treatments and placements and programs you didn't want to be part of. I was searching for answers constantly. I'm sorry if I gave you too much love and if I gave you too little. I loved you every second of every day without ceasing. I'm sorry if I couldn't convey it consistently, if I didn't know how to lovingly support you when your symptoms created chaos and stole the child I knew. I'm sorry if I reacted to the symptoms without considering your own suffering, when I should have been reacting to the person. You're my son, and I loved you.

But it was hard not to get enmeshed with your illness. I couldn't have a good day unless you had a good day. But now I can see that you often had no choice and that's because I didn't give you one. I thought I was keeping you alive, and I thought through this I was showing you love, by fighting for you, by getting you every service I could find. I suffered so much from your diagnosis, and I displayed it. I'm sorry for that because you were the one who truly was suffering. You didn't choose schizophrenia. But I could have chosen to make you more of a partner and less of a "mental patient." I was fierce, and you were gentle, always, and my ferocity intimidated you. I knew it at the time, but I didn't know how to love you without being completely and overwhelmingly fierce. My heart was willing, but my skill was nil.

I wish I had turned a more loving face toward you every day—love that was absent of angst and anxiety and fright and aggression. I told you every day I was proud of you. But did I show it?

I'm sorry if my compassion was compromised when you probably needed it most. When I was literally one of your only friends left after illness drove all others away, why did I find it so hard to dig deeper for compassion? Why did I find it difficult to be there every hour of the day for you? For months, you called me at least 20 times a day while I was at work, preoccupied with job tasks and worried about how you were doing while I was 50 miles away, and I answered the phone sharply sometimes. Because you only ever asked, repeatedly, "When will you be home?"

I couldn't handle the expectation to be your only everything, to answer the same questions patiently 20 times in eight hours, while wondering if I could keep this job with the many absences the illness caused, with all the emotional upheaval the illness created for me. I couldn't get you to stop calling, but did I have to be rude about it? I was overwhelmed by your illness and felt defeated by our medicalized, increasingly smaller lives. When it was just "you and me against the world," did I make you feel like it was just you and not "we"? I regret that, with every living cell in my being.

I'm sorry for not understanding what you may have needed. And, not understanding it, I failed to provide it. I frequently surmised that you were capable of more than you were, and I was frequently wrong. I also thought you were less capable than you were, and again, I was frequently wrong. It's very difficult to discern in an illness that drastically affects behavior, what is illness and what is behavior. Were you doing all you could, for yourself, to aid in recovery? Were you a spoiled child, as some suggested, manipulating me, or were you exhibiting symptoms of your illness?

These are not things parents should be the experts on. We are tasked with guiding and aiding a very sick person in an illness we barely understand, with no medical training and very little real support, all while grieving the child who has disappeared into psychosis. A lot of clinicians don't have a great understanding of schizophrenia, either, as I've come to realize. I only had the help that I had. And I was deathly afraid of making a mistake, which led me to make many. I have studied schizophrenia copiously since your passing. It was knowledge that I needed much, much earlier. It's not an excuse, but still, I am sorry.

One day shortly before your death you called from your apartment and asked if we could go get dinner. I was exhausted from work and seven years of upheaval and illness, and I said no. You kept asking "Why? Why not, Mom?" And I just kept saying, "Because I'm tired and I just need a night off. I need time off this," I told you. You didn't get time off schizophrenia, which you didn't point out to me, but I pointed out my need to you. You finally said, "Please, Mom?"

I would give my proverbial right arm today to rescind that decision. When I'm on my deathbed from whatever illness finally takes me, I will be crying out for forgiveness for this. It's one of the most painful regrets I have. You didn't get a single minute off of a terrible illness that completely devastated your life, but I did. And I chose time off over spending two additional hours with you. And then I told you about it. There's no way to tell you how sorry I am for that.

Finally, I am sorry if I didn't lead with kindness every day. I am reminded by a photo I took of a wall in our house where I'd written in giant marker the days of the week and your chores for that day. Today, this photo crushes me. I thought I'd found a clever way to avoid arguments about doing something productive during the day while I worked. Ugh. I thought if I created an objective list, you would respond to the list and not the drama of an argument.

I tell parents in my support group now, "Always first be kind to, before being critical of, your sick child." That's a better lesson than the one I was trying to impart about responsibility.

And if others take anything away from this brief essay, I hope it's this one: Each day, in every way you can, the face you show to your child should be one of kindness first. There is time enough for lessons on responsibility and diligence and working hard. With that time gone for me with the loss of my son, these are so many lessons I'd hoped to impart that meant absolutely nothing. And the only lesson that matters now is kindness.

Only kindness matters. It's a lesson I hope no one else helping a sick child ever has to learn.

Laura Pogliano *is a training and education consultant in Baltimore, MD. She was the primary caretaker of her son, Zaccaria, who was stricken with schizophrenia at age 17. Ms. Pogliano is the director of Families For Treatment, a Baltimore non-profit that provides practical supports and small grants to the caregivers of those with mental illnesses and their families. Her son's story has been featured on CBS News, in USA Today, in Oprah Magazine, and in Baltimore Magazine. Her son's story was also featured in a documentary called* Shattered Families, *which won numerous awards on the independent film circuit. Ms. Pogliano is passionate about helping families understand how to best help their loved ones and improving patient care and outcomes. She has also been a co-host of the mental health podcast,* Revealing Voices, *with Pastor Tony Roberts.*

Crystal Glass

Leanne Sype

Dear H.,

You once asked me if you are a "glass child." As in a child who is fragile, requires careful attention and handling, and requires extra expense, all due to your mental health disorders. You asked me the question with your eyes clouded in concern and worry in your voice, as if maybe being a glass child was a burden.

My immediate reaction as your mother was to reassure you that you are no burden to me. "Of course not!" I replied to you. As the weeks have passed, though, I haven't been able to stop thinking about your question. The more I think about glass, the more I realize how very much like glass you are.

I should have asked you, "What's so bad about glass?" Because you, my sweet girl, are like crystal glass. A most exquisite and beautiful form of glass that has the ability to refract light, shining brilliant colors back into the world for us to behold. Crystal is both strong and fragile, crafted with noticeable strength yet easy to shatter when mishandled. There is no human who isn't shattered when crashed into the depths of loss, grief, turmoil, and the darkness of depression and suicidal thoughts.

You are not "expensive." You are priceless. You are worth more than the most prized crystal glass sitting in a fancy museum somewhere. And every dime I spend, every minute I spend, every emotional ounce I spend taking care of you, your brain, and your life, will never come close to how much you are worth to me.

Are your mental illness symptoms hard sometimes? Yes. Are you, as a whole, precious person with radiant perspective, love, empathy, and compassion, like the most exquisite piece of crystal glass I've ever seen?

Yes, sweet girl. You are my brilliant glass child. A wonder to behold. I love you to pieces, whether you are whole or shattered. You are priceless.

Love,
Mom

Leanne Sype *is a mother of two teens, both with mental health diagnoses. She's a mental health awareness advocate in her community, sharing her story with other parents to help normalize mental illness, treatments, and recovery. Leanne's goal in her community work is to encourage families to advocate for their loved ones and empower their loved ones to engage in treatment for long-term mental wellness.*

Ripples of Hope
Leslie Carpenter

Dear Son,

There are so many things I wish I could tell you and share with you that seem impossible now because of the cruelties of your very severe illness.

First, I am so very sorry that you got sick. This wasn't your fault. I know you blame me because we learned, after you got sick, that there is a history of mental illness in my family with my dad and others. I get it. It's fair to be angry because I didn't know when we decided to have children.

Second, I so wish we had been able to find treatment for you that you would accept in ways that were less traumatic than going to the emergency department at the hospital so many times. I wish you could someday understand just how scared we were to lose you when you were suicidal and suffering so. We hoped to find you compassionate, effective treatment to help you suffer less.

Third, I wish we could have found effective treatment that treated both your Schizoaffective illness and your substance use disorder at the same time, in the same place. I wish you could have had the insight to recognize that marijuana only puts you back into psychosis, over and over again.

I know you have suffered from your illness and felt so alone. I know it hurts you deeply that we could no longer have you live with us in our home. And yet, you just kept deteriorating while you were with us, and we clearly couldn't help you to stay in treatment on our own. It became untenable for us to have you in our home. It broke our hearts to make this decision, but we knew, in the long run, that it was best to try to find you a better living situation where you could have the support you needed to be able to have your best chance at living your best life. We also know that we will not always be here, and we wanted to give you your best chance for after we are gone.

Finally, because you so resented our turning to NAMI (the National Alliance on Mental Illness) and doing any advocacy, we haven't let you know the extent of our advocacy on your behalf. You have seemed to resent any time we give to anyone else, including your sister and your grandfather. And so, we have not shared the extent of our advocacy to make things better for you and also for everyone else living with serious brain illnesses. I actually ended up retiring in 2019, to spend the rest of my life working to improve the mental illness treatment system and do this in a number of different ways. You don't know it, but you are in my heart with every talk I give, every bill I advocate for, the five years of work to create Iowa's first AOT (Assisted Outpatient Treatment) Program, every email I write and every Op Ed I submit. I do this for you, even though I know you will likely never realize it.

Your illness has changed you and I miss the sweet little boy who so loved to sit on the couch with me and let me read books to you. I know you are in there, somewhere beneath or within, and I hope someday you can know that you are loved. We so often tell you and hug you at each visit, but I am not sure you believe us.

Were I to create a better world for you, it would have absolutely no mental illnesses in it and no suffering. No drugs either. Just the ability to enjoy yourself with no need for any substance of any kind.

Your dad and I love you, even when we have to set boundaries.

We hope someday you know and believe this, deeply within your heart.

With love, forever and always,
Mom

Leslie Carpenter *retired early from her physical therapy career to do SMI advocacy on a local, state, and national basis. She is a public speaker and a lobbyist in the Iowa Legislature, serves on multiple advisory boards and the NAMI Iowa Board of Directors, teaches NAMI Provider, and recently started Iowa's first AOT program.*

My Dearest Birdy
Linda Flynn

My Dearest Birdy,

I know that isn't the name I gave you but one you have chosen to adopt. It's been 16 months since I have heard from you. That day when you told me you never wanted to see or hear from me again and refused all financial support was one of the worst of my life.

I think of you and miss you every single day. I know you are living unhoused thousands of miles away and I wonder every day if you are warm, dry, and have access to food. I hope with every fiber of my being that you are treated with kindness, but I know that is unlikely. I do all I can for homeless people here. I advocate, I look them in the eyes, and I help. Every face I see is yours.

I wrote to you every Sunday even though I know that you don't do email anymore, but it helps me channel my love.

I wait every day for that phone call that you have left this world, and it's like losing you over and over again.

I love you my beautiful child, and I miss you.

Love,
Mom

Linda Flynn *is a Canadian executive working in post-secondary education and has recently begun sharing her story and working to bring a voice to families like hers. Linda's 30-year-old son, who has suffered from serious mental illness since he was a young adult, severed all ties with his family and has been homeless and missing since November 2021.*

I Carry You Within My Heart

Linda Oatman High

Dear Zach,

I carried you beneath my heart, and since August of 1990, I have carried you within my heart. You were the best little boy, always so full of love and joy. You played baseball and football and basketball. You wrestled. You played piano and bass guitar. You were in Cub Scouts. We traveled, and we swam with dolphins. You and I went skiing at Smuggler's Notch, and we attended concerts together. We laughed . . . so much. You were always lots of fun to be around.

When you became ill in October of 2014, I was so consumed by confusion and grief and helplessness. The diagnosis of schizophrenia hit me like a freight train, and there were times I thought that I could no longer go on, now that my sweet son was sick. It's been a rollercoaster nine years, with too many hospitalizations, medication changes, doctors, and stress. If someone had told me back when you were a child that we'd be in this situation, I never would have believed it. Yet here we are.

I think we've come a long way. You are (at times) accepting the diagnosis, accepting the illness, accepting the fact that medication will always be necessary. I'm accepting (at times) the fact that my beloved youngest son has a brain disease. I can talk about it without crying (sometimes), and I can write about it. I've realized that, despite your illness, I can still laugh, I can still pursue my own passions, and I can feel joy.

Sometimes I wonder if devastation such as we've experienced actually helps one to somehow feel even more joy, because we realize just how precious that happiness can be. There are times (most days, in fact) that I become irritable and short-tempered with the symptoms. It's the sickness that annoys me; I freaking hate this illness. I am (some days) bitter and jaded and angry at whatever Higher Power might (or might not) exist. I question a God who could allow a human being to suffer in this way.

If I could take it from you, I would . . . in a heartbeat, in a breath. I'm thankful for all the joy we've shared, and I'm so grateful for the people that you've brought into my life. Ironically, the people with whom I'm the closest are all people who came into my life and my heart through you. If there is a Plan, or Fate, or some mysterious Higher Power in charge of this chaotic mess, I can see that the one plus, the pro among all the cons, is these people, these humans that I love so very much. I thank you for them.

I thank you for your heart, which is still (most days) caring and kind and open. I thank you for your willingness to get up each and every morning and face this illness. I know how hard you fight, and I think you are one of the bravest men I know.

I asked you one time if you are angry to have schizophrenia, and you said no. I'm angry, though. I'm angry that you have to carry this burden, that you often don't feel well enough to laugh, that you're so, so tired. I'm angry that my free-spirited little boy no longer exists. I don't want to be angry, but I am. However, I'm also thankful. I'm grateful for you, for your life, for your breath, for your heart that still beats bravely. I'm thankful to be your mom, and I'll always be here for you.

I'll always love you . . . no matter what. I carried you beneath my heart, and I carry you within my heart. We will continue to face this and to fight this, together. Forever. I love you to the moon and back, and you know that I'm a very determined person. Please keep fighting, and I will, too.

Love,
Mom

To Peter and Moms Like Me

Lindsay Dawn

To: Peter and moms like me,

In 2002, when I first learned that I was going to be a mom, I was full of so many emotions, as most moms-to-be are, but my emotions were different. Or were they? I was simply terrified. Not scared of the pain, the nausea, the swelling, no fear related to changes in life, no worries about finances. Nope. My irrational fear was that I would have a child like my brother.

My brother Peter was a difficult child. No affect until he was nearly two years old, no babbling or talking until nearly two years old, and then it was full sentences. Consistently defiant, manipulative at a young age, no remorse, enjoyed watching others suffer, and loved fire. This is not just my parents' recollection but mine as well. My brother unintentionally gave me an education in mental illness at an early age. So, I didn't feel my fear was irrational at all.

But then... then the day came when I saw my baby boy. It was technically the day after he was born due to me being sick post-op, but it didn't matter. (Although I do believe that the lack of bonding affected us later.) I was in love. My fear of having a child like Peter was silenced, at least temporarily. Landon was born on November 22nd, 2002, at approximately 4:40 pm via c-section. He was about 19 days early because of my high blood pressure, and ironically enough the size of his noggin. The doctors, upon reviewing the ultrasound, said that I would never have him naturally, hence the early birthday. The size of his head did play a role in testing later in his life. It was the best day of my life to that point. There was nothing I would not do for this child.

Once Landon was around 15 months old, the silence I had been enjoying vanished. Landon was beginning to show behaviors that something was not quite right. By this point, the fear I once had resumed exactly where it had left off. This was just the start of Landon's long journey into a world filled with lots of testing, so many questions and evaluations, and too few answers.

Over the years, there have been too many diagnoses to mention, and this is partially due to no one wanting to give my child a diagnosis that was formulated for an adult. I understood. But I was also frustrated and confused and angry. But we kept going—trudging along to various doctors and therapists and taking medications that were supposed to be helping. By the time my son was nine years old, we had tried at least five different medications, he was suicidal three times and attempted once, and had been evaluated more than half a dozen times by various clinicians. Yes, you read that correctly. My child was suicidal three times before the age of ten, and an attempt survivor. Those were the days I did not know if I could keep doing this parenting thing. Not long after Landon turned nine, his father and I divorced. This changed the dynamic for several years.

At 15 years old, Landon moved from his father's home and came to live with me, my then-boyfriend, and Landon's brother, Karston. While the change was significant, the challenges were plentiful. Landon had not been taking his medication and was in a state of "I don't need medicine" when he came to live with us. As a mom, I knew better and so the next leg of our journey began. Since that time, nearly four years ago, Landon has flourished on numerous levels, and I am so proud to be his mom. I cannot pick one time—however, I will say that he is constantly surprising me with the effort he has applied to do better and be better.

Landon's journey with his mental health will never be over. There is not a destination. There will be pit-stops, rest areas, traffic jams, overnight stays away from home, flat tires, and engine troubles, but he will never be alone. Landon has an amazing family and support system in place and when you are traveling a journey such as a severe mental illness, family and support are priceless.

The Most Powerful Event

Lisa Ashley

What was the most powerful life event you have ever experienced?

Getting a great job?

Falling in love?

Buying your first house?

Having a child?

Having a child with a serious mental illness?

That's my event. Never in my wildest dreams did I ever think I would have a child with SMI. Absolutely not on my radar. Some kind of addiction most likely, since that was in the family history, maybe depression too. But Schizophrenia?

I always wanted children and all the dreams that go with that. As they grow, you help keep them safe and healthy. You want them to be successful and happy and find their way in this world as an adult. But parents of children like my son lose that dream child forever. The one that was so incredibly bright getting into seven colleges/universities and not making it through their first year. Then BAM! You all hit the wall and suddenly enter the world of the Serious Mentally Ill.

The world of numerous 5150s, hospitalizations, jail, homelessness, meds, no meds, and erratic behaviors, just to start. Let's not forget about all your tears, too.

However, for my son, after 12 years of riding the roller coaster, we are one of the lucky ones for now. We have hit a sweet spot, a glimmer of hope. He has been stable on meds for almost three years now. He takes his meds daily, lives with me, and meets with his case manager and doctors regularly. And after 13 years of unemployment, he now has a part-time job.

I belong to a Buddhist meditation group that has kept me grounded for several years. Most serious practitioners have mentors or teachers to guide them. I was asked once to be on one of their panels to talk about my practice. Someone asked me, "Who is your teacher?" I answered, "My son is my teacher. My beautiful son teaches me about love, patience, understanding, strength, and courage. But above all, he has taught me about hope."

One must never give up on hope.

Lisa Ashley writes, *"I am a retired pediatric nurse practitioner, the mother of two beautiful young men. I live in Sacramento, California, although I was born in Massachusetts. My favorite thing to do is gardening and enjoying beautiful days with friends and family."*

To My WHOLE-Hearted Son
Lori Reho

Thank you for giving me new eyes to see.

April 16, 1993, the breath of the Divine filled your tender body, and you became one with humanity—my second and last time assisting God in the co-creation of life. You filled the room with sweet smells of a newborn miracle, and I thanked God for you. I glimpsed your soul that day as our eyes locked in a gaze of wonder and curiosity about each other. That moment has never left me. I saw then what I was able to see through the eyes and heart of my 21 experienced and difficult years.

Watching you sprout into boyhood was like opening a new gift every day. You carried laughter and buoyancy with every energetic movement you made, and dull moments were strangers to our home. You lived life with your whole heart, and it was bigger than your body. At age eight, you revealed concerns of ruminations, yet my eyes could only see a happy, healthy boy.

Without delay, adolescence appeared and your love for music matured into a single-focused blissful passion, while your dreaming morphed into visioning. The perpetual shenanigans with friends were heart-stopping to say the least, but your contagious laughter as you explained your behavior could melt away my intolerance. Music became the heart of our home, and I found happiness when I danced to the beat of your drum. I was blessed with daily immersions into the rhythmic sounds that flowed from your bedroom, still unaware that you were lost somewhere between the melodies and the riffs, soothing the disturbances that had burrowed inside of your mind. Your first band became your first love, and you wrote songs late into the night and wrote with your whole heart.

At age 15, you said something was wrong with your brain and 24 hours after the prescribed tranquilizers we administered, you were unrecognizable. I held you tight in my arms that day as we agreed this was not the solution. My eyes saw a puberty-stricken, handsome young man with big dreams and a temporary hormone imbalance.

As high school faded into memory and your circle of connections dimmed, I grew curious about the next steps on your path to adulthood. The band had dissolved, and love took hold of your heart until the summer of 2016. At age 23, your heart was bruised and your relationship dreams were shattered. That event induced the introduction of yourself to yourself. That summer the protective veil between the emotional and the physiological was lifted, and the two worlds collided. That summer changed the course of our lives. Fetal position became your new normal and sleep was a long-lost friend. Doctors, research, tests, money, medications, journals, tears, hospitals, and more tests, bedside prayers, more tears, workdays without sleep, paralyzing nightmares, and crippling anxiety were just a sample of our new reality. The vibrations and tones of music had ceased, and you sold your instruments. Friends and family vanished in confusion and fear. The little rest to be treasured was accompanied by the sounds of pounding hearts and weeping. You had your first psychotic break. My eyes only saw a broken heart.

The next five years brought us closer together and yet further apart than we had ever been. As any mother would do, I swiftly mastered the art of integrating new roles into my personhood as you were trying desperately to understand who you were. In some ways I was meeting you for the first time all over again. I will never forget sitting at your bedside one night when once again our eyes locked once again in a gaze of wonder and curiosity about each other just like at birth. This gaze, however, was filled with questions and confusion, yet still without words affirmed our commitment as mother and child to hold hope for a beautiful and fulfilling life. Again, I got a glimpse of your soul, and, yes, it was still Divine.

For years we existed in an ebb and flow of trust and mistrust, love and anger, fear and then determination. We came together with expectation, and we even stopped talking to each other at times. You researched and journaled; I joined support groups and counseling. We both put full intention and responsibility into a solution for living, and you did it with your whole heart.

The engulfing desperation to normalize led you to the frequently traveled road of mind-altering substances, where addiction claimed custody of your brain. Of course, it never kept its promise to solve all your problems and ultimately intensified the symptoms you were trying to fight. I threw every lesson I knew at you and imposed every solution I could think of. I always tried to stay one step ahead and usually landed one step behind. My love for you, which knew no boundaries, began to cause me deep pain, disappointment, and resentment until I realized I was loving you to death through my codependency and all I really needed to do was to love you. You were not broken and did not need to be fixed. You are the exact you that you were created to be and finally I had the eyes to see.

Walking this journey has allowed me to see with the eyes of compassion and acceptance. I am awake, and I now realize that our hearts are the essence of our being. Although your brain has experienced change, your heart is still the same whole heart. So long as the breath of God remains in your tender body, there is a hope and purpose for your life. I accept the perfect you that you are, and I know that every decision you make is part of your own story, and I do not have a right to change the narrative.

I love you with my whole heart!
Mom

Lori Reho *is a pastoral counselor who has a private practice in Tampa, FL, where she offers counseling, leadership coaching, and mindfulness training. She has also built a career in medical administration and works* *as a practice administrator for a surgical practice in Sarasota. Lori has lived with Joey for 30 years, and also has a daughter who lives in North Carolina with her husband and four children. Lori is a devoted mother and Nana and is involved in peer support groups for moms with adult children who have mental health challenges.*

Dear Joey
The Reverend Dr. James Reho

Dear Joey,

The day I told you that I was going to propose to your mother, I didn't expect any reaction. I already knew you well, well enough to know that you shunned touch. I had read that people with your constellation of diagnoses were not typically affectionate or even capable of sustaining interest in others. Yet that day, without reservation, you hugged me in a deep, loving embrace. You welcomed me to the family. That day, we chose each other, you and I. I chose to come into our family, knowing that you suffered from multiple mental disorders and that you would likely live with us or need some level of support for a lifetime. You chose to accept me into your very small inner circle and gave me your trust and faith and continual candor, for a lifetime.

I came into your life in my 40s, with you half my age, already in your 20s. All the "used-to-be's" of your past that people would tell me about, or show me in photos—how you used to be so lively, so much fun, so thoughtful . . . I missed all that. When others in the family express their love of how you used to be—before your psychotic break, before the isolation, voices, hospitalizations, paranoia and delusions, manic exploits, medication, and resultant addiction—I am just silent. I didn't know you then. I wasn't there for those sweet Christmas mornings of childhood, for your first bike or middle school pranks and jokes, or for your teenage band and early loves. While others could love you for who you were...I can only love you for who you are.

We have had struggles over the years. There has been anger and frustration, the testing of limits and boundaries, judgment, and resentment. Sometimes I would say that you were my greatest spiritual teacher, because in living with you I come face-to-face with my own defects of character in ways I've never known before. Learning to live with you as your mental state fluctuated from season to season has been a fierce journey of love. Your mother and I were not split apart by these stressors but became even more closely bonded. Each of us has had to "dig deep" and come to greater and greater self-awareness and greater and greater communion with one another. This is a gift, though at times it came in challenging packaging.

You and I have always been kind to each other, yet each of us, I know, has had to deal with the soreness of resentment and anger with one another, too. Yet we have also shared moments of intimate conversation, honest self-revelation, and real "male bonding" lifting weights or working on music together. You are the son I never had, and I do love you for who you are.

As I've come to know you, I've come to know that you are lovable and valuable for who you are today. You don't need all the "used-to-be's" to be worthy of love. You are made in the image and likeness of God, and that includes all of you, just like it includes all of me. That means God is not absent from your being because of your mental illness. There is nothing "wrong" with how you are, with who you are. I used to think that you in your disorder were more selfish and self-centered than others. I'm no longer sure of that. Perhaps you just have fewer filters and more honesty than most. Very few of us humans truly evolve beyond being kind self-seekers.

Over the years, I've found so much to love in who you are: You are someone who strives for excellence in your music; you are someone who seeks a partner to love and serve and with whom to share life's journey; you are someone who cuddles the dog; will help when asked; and has dreams and aspirations. I don't know if those will come true, or if you will find the love and right-fitting place you seek in this world. I don't know if you see yourself as lovable or if you still believe in yourself and in your dreams. I hope so. And I hope I have helped you know that you are lovable, valuable, and worth believing in. No longer do I think that your mental disorders can be magically erased by the "right" doctor or medicine or therapy. Yet, no longer do I think that they must be erased for you to be productively journeying on your path of life. Your disorders are part of your story, a big part of your path, but these diagnoses and conditions are not all that you are.

Joey, my son, I love you for who you are, right now, today. I am grateful to you for being a spiritual teacher for me, although you have no idea that you serve in this role. I am grateful for our relationship, for the interests we share, and for the moments when we are just two men who care for each other. I am grateful for the life we live together and for your hug that day, many years ago, when we chose each other. I choose you again, today.

With love,
James
Your grateful stepdad

James Reho *is an Episcopal priest who serves as pastor of a small and sweet church in Southwest Florida. He has lived with Joey since marrying Joey's mom Lori in 2017. He is a writer and a yoga practitioner and enjoys gardening and playing several musical instruments, most recently the five-string banjo. Before studying for the priesthood, James was on the chemistry faculty at East Carolina University, where he taught Physical Chemistry and directed the undergraduate laboratory program.*

Our Journey Together

Mara Briere, MA, CFLE

Dear C,

We have traveled a difficult journey together, and I am a richer person because of it.

Your struggles began when you were too young, and they dogged you in one form or another throughout your life. PTSD. Bipolar. Substance Use. Schizoaffective. Each challenge was met with your capacity and willingness to understand, grow, and develop a resilience that is awesome.

It has been hard to witness your brain disease and traumatic brain injury impact you. You are truly a walking miracle. That last suicide attempt ironically gave you a new life. I will never forget that night when the staff at the group home called and told me that you were being airlifted to Brigham & Women's as a no-name. I had gone to the group home earlier that day to pick up an award for being so involved with you. I told the staff that you were symptomatic and psychotic and to keep an eye on you. They believed your act more than they believed me, even after giving me an award because of how well I know you! You have always been so good at masking your symptoms. I became an expert in seeing through you.

Six weeks in the critical care unit, two months on a medical floor, many surgeries, so many decisions I had to make in honoring you and your wishes (The Five Wishes saved both of us) and then 2+ years at a state hospital, first in rehab and then in the locked psych unit. Then to another group home. Several relapses, a short hospital stay, and finally the combination of supportive residential living, outpatient treatment, and a better understanding of what you needed to do to stay alive, remain in the community, and live your best life.

You have become an effective peer recovery counselor. You live independently with great community supports. You have friends. You have meaningful work. You are teaching yourself to cook.

You came out of it all with your heart and personality intact. You walk! Truly a miracle on all counts.

You ask me why I continue to hang in with you. You are my beloved child. I adore the adult you are. And you shine a bright light into dark places. You make me a better person.

Throughout all the heartache, disappointment, and the discouraging times, we grew our bond and strengthened it with ongoing support, understanding, and mutual love.

All my love always,
M

Mara Briere writes, *"I have been surrounded by serious mental illness throughout my life, personally and professionally. When both my daughters were diagnosed with serious mental illnesses, I founded a nonprofit organization, Grow a Strong Family, for supporters to acquire the tools they need to advocate and promote healthier families."*

To My Youngest Son and Middle Child

Mary Renz

My youngest son and middle child,

You developed paranoid schizophrenia at the age of 18. Your first break came two weeks after your high school graduation. NAMI did not exist at this time. You and I had a very close son/mother relationship before this first break. I believe in hindsight that we had a joint purpose in life. Thus, I prayed that God would make me be the person I needed to be to interact with you and guide and direct my every step. God did just that, but God let me experience the reality of paranoid schizophrenia through my son.

After the first 13 years, you finally got the opportunity for Clozapine in September of 1997. You went from a halfway house to a group home to an apartment with a roommate to your own apartment in about a two-year span at Life Help, a Fountain House Model. You were in remission and never returned to the state hospital. You were responsible for taking your medication, available only in pill form, and going for the test every other week.

You enjoyed the next 11 years of this life. You got a job, but the minute the employer learned of your illness, he found a reason to let you go. This word traveled fast in a small town, so you could not get employment.

You were able to play golf again, so you've played in all the charity golf tournaments with me paying an entry fee. In high school, your golf team won third place in the 4A state tournament in Texas. You sported a two-handicap at the time. Since remission, you have a four-handicap. You had two holes in one before becoming ill.

You could drive home for weekends. You were very grateful for all we had done, and you expressed it to me. When you were in your right mind, you even agreed with the involuntary commitments. I love you so much and I am so proud to have been your mother.

You could no longer take Clozapine in Sept. of 2008, and somehow got the "superbug" MRSA that took your life on November 11, 2008 at age 43. You live in my heart. I am forever grateful to God for your life and the honor to be your mother.

Mary Renz writes, *"I submitted because our journey was in another time and this shows it was better in an earlier time. I hope it will give hope to families that America can do better and has, in an earlier time. These Brain Disorders are very individualized, meaning what works for one is no guarantee it will work for another. Clozapine is the gold standard and everyone who has schizophrenia should have the opportunity to see if it works for them."*

The Pregnancy Journal

Mary DiNardi

Dear Justin,

I recently found the journal I kept while I was pregnant with you. I cried reading it. I never would have imagined how hard your life, our lives, would be. Our journey is not the one I wrote about in that journal. The hopes and dreams I had then are different from the ones I have now.

I know I've told you before, but you saved my life. The love I had for you pushed me to leave the abusive situation we were in. I'm not sure if I would have made it out alive if I didn't have you then. I thank the Universe for putting you in my life; she knew we needed each other.

I can't believe you will be 29 in just a few weeks. Sometimes it feels like just yesterday that you were a toddler playing in the dirt with your Matchbox cars. Other times, it feels like we have been on this journey together for at least 60 years.

We have had some happy days, some average days, some hard days, and some super scary and exhausting days. But one constant has been my unconditional love for you. There has not been a day that has gone by that I haven't loved you. Yes, there have been challenging days when I haven't liked your choices, your behavior, the way you have treated me and others, but I still loved you. I loved you on your best day and on your worst. I laughed with you and cried with you. I literally talked you out of jumping off a bridge several years ago. And after they took you to the hospital, I took 15 minutes to regroup and then I went to work. Not because I wanted to, but because I needed to (as a single mom). Boy, we have had some tough days! But I have never left your side.

Just this past Christmas was tough for us. Our family was faced with illness and uncertainty. You were scared. This caused you to unleash on the one closest to you. You became angry and said hurtful things. You vowed never to talk to me again. Yet. . . I still loved you. Don't get me wrong, my heart was crushed in a way that I wasn't sure it would ever recover from. But I'm here and always will be.

I'm so grateful for you, Justin. I'm blessed to be your mom. So while our lives look nothing like how I imagined them in my journal years ago, I'm grateful that we have the opportunity to rewrite it. As hard as our journey is, it is our journey, and I'm blessed to be on it with you. I love you!

Love always,
Mom

For the past several years, **Mary DiNardi** *has worked on obtaining mental health resources for her community and in raising awareness for the suicide crisis. Mary wants you to know her son is more than his diagnosis. Justin is extremely bright, funny, and strong. She is blessed to be his mom.*

Dear Most Beloved Son

Seetha Sundararamen

Dear Most Beloved Son,

I am trying my best to love you just as you love me so unconditionally and freely.

I know that your world is a tad bit different than mine. I either slide back to my past or escape to the future, where you are in the all-glorious present. I am indeed immensely grateful for you agreeing to take medicines to handle your delusions and depression. If not, I would not get to meet the most sweet and enchanting young man you are.

I wish you to enjoy all the joy and happiness that this life has to offer. It is incredibly tough on some days, wild and tumultuous, dictated by sheer brain chemistry—yet sublime and peaceful on some days. It is for periods of peace and quietness which we aim and live for.

The calm follows the storm many times in your case. It is very tough for me to explain my feelings and love towards you. I can only feel that, and I wish not to be drowned in that, lest I lose sight of true love. It is tough and hard at times, and I thank you for trusting me so deeply.

I pray (if there is a benevolent soul up and out there or in?) that the medicines you take and the sports you play help you keep anchored in life so that you may enjoy all that life has to offer you.

The Fish Catcher

Sherry Lanning

Arriving at the fishpond, we saw a duck family.

"Those are my brother's kids!" you said assuredly.

"Really," I smirked.

"You're smiling at me mom! I love it when you smile at me!"

My 50-year-old, fish-catching son, off to drown some worms.

We named you Robin, meaning "bright and shining fame." The perfect name for our 7 ½ pounds of potential. Within the next 12 years, you would be joined by three sisters and three brothers.

Our family of nine was musical, performing annually at local fairs. Your spontaneous energy enhanced our group.

March 21, 1986

At 13, Robin is filled with life! His heart is as big as the sea. He loves pizza, basketball, and fishing. He sings like an angel.

While competing at your school's State Convention, you placed first in vocal solo. Your dynamic performance received a standing ovation. Your bright shining moment—until the music stopped!

Once animated, your face turned masklike. Your ebony eyes stared broodingly. You were 15, banging your head against walls.

We took you for assessment, leaving you behind locked doors at a psych unit. It felt like we had left you at the dog pound. Your diagnosis was depression—unfortunately, missing your prodromal phase of schizophrenia.

I was attending nursing school, learning about mental illness while your hard-working dad kept us supported. Your siblings compensated as they could, often over-achieving.

Our previous idealism had been challenged. We couldn't fit you into our fundamentalist formulas. As your stability floundered, your care was "assumed" by the State. During this time you "went missing." You were 20, too old for milk carton ads for missing children and before cell phones. The police found you in Myrtle Beach, South Carolina, surviving on the streets.

August 23, 1992

I clung to my simple, solid faith. "Jesus, let me lay my head in Your lap, and whisper my deepest fears without someone scolding (Fear is a sin!). You say, 'Can a mother forget her child?' Give me courage to remember him. If his loss is eternal, he will have lived briefly in my heart. And Jesus, no matter what, I'll always lay my head in Your lap."

You met JoAnn, staying together several years in North Carolina, tending horses.

At 30, you were committed to the Oregon State Hospital where One Flew Over the Cuckoo's Nest was filmed. Visitation was bleak indeed. Human souls shuffled like robots; vacant eyes stared while mouths drooled their morning meds.

I'd exit that institution resolved to "fix something." I resorted to pulling random weeds sprouting from the sidewalk.

Schizophrenia was diagnosed at last. Clozapine expanded your speech from monosyllables to sentences—tragically, 15 years too late, as psychotic assaults are cumulative, degenerating the brain, resulting in chronic illness.

Later, you were transferred to another facility. Over time you would stay in approximately 20 facilities.

Once your siblings left home, I pursued disaster nursing with medical missions to Haiti, Guatemala, and Uganda. Inspired by the resilience of those afflicted, my capacity to care for you increased.

Returning from Guatemala, I heard you had gone missing again. The police posted your endangered persons report on my birthday. "Voices" had lured you back to Myrtle Beach, promising you a job! Hopes for employment prompted a coast-to-coast bus ride.

Once again, you were found by police, only to be "caught and released" to unsupervised group homes, increasing your delusions, causing you to sleep behind dumpsters.

The ER gave occasional respite. I'd cradle your head as you sprawled on the floor. My tormented child—nicotine and fear infused your sweat, permeating the padded room. Instinctively, I'd rock you like a baby.

Just in time, your father saved us both. He had begun to understand schizophrenia, realizing your brain was disordered. We decided to bring you home. With God's help, we would manage your care together, one day at a time. As you complied with your meds, our home became your refuge.

Late one night, I heard singing from your room. "Rise Again" by Dallas Holm. "Cause I'll rise again, ain't no power on Earth can tie me down. Yes, I'll rise again, death can't keep me in the ground!"

After years of silence, your voice had returned with a vengeance.

In the morning, you stuffed your backpack with yesterday's worms, sodas, and smokes. Your "fish catching" status was proudly announced by three fishing poles while you waited for the bus.

Reporting to the pond, you made your first cast, hoping to catch Michelle—your old girlfriend turned fish. She fussed hard getting caught so you tossed her back until tomorrow when she'd be less fickle.

At night, you shuffled home saying, "Michelle's sure getting fat!"

I said, "Welcome home, son. Your dad's made soup."

You said, "Right on! That sounds good."

Having taken your fistful of meds, you tread to bed.

"Are you warm enough son?" I asked.

"Yes, Mom."

I said, "We love you Robin. We're glad you're home safe."

"Right on!" you said.

Special Olympics renewed your interest in basketball, softball, and bowling. Your natural athleticism remains apparent to all.

Mother's Day was sweetened by your gift of two cans of Almond Roca. My birthday was remembered with a rosebush, yellow, which you planted.

Your previous Mother's Day card read, "If you treat your sons like heroes, they'll become heroes, if only in your own eyes."

Robin, of bright and shining fame, you are my hero.

Forever Your Mother,
Sherry Lanning, RN/retired

Sherry Lanning *is a retired nurse living in Oregon. Along with her husband, David, they care for their son Robin, challenged by schizophrenia.*

Harrison
Anonymous

Harrison,
The first paragraph is a poem I wrote for you. The rest is just for you.

From an outsider looking in . . . As you wake to the daily misleading, intrusive thoughts, apprehension and doubts set in. Burdened by demanding, time-consuming rituals that guide you with daunting motivations to make it just right. As you grapple with understanding the true nature of the present, false illusions of reality, fear, and avoidance creep in, finding their way through the cracks of once-happy moments. Despair taking hold of seemingly easy tasks. Words of desperation take control, trapping you into isolation. Friend or foe, left or right, to do or not to do, fight or flight? Controlled and exhausted! My dream and prayers for you would be that one day OCD would be a thing of the past and that you could live your best life carefree of the fears and rituals.

I salute you for the courage it takes to fight the invisible fight with the one that has the audacity to invade your life. The one that wants so desperately to hold on to you, to hold you down, to control you. Please know OCD cannot win. Your resilience and determination are above all and will prevail. You are stronger than you know. God has given you the power to defeat the enemy. He has equipped you with extreme talents only designed for you, brains that can outsmart the cleverest, a laugh that is infectious. You have charisma and charm, such a gorgeous young man. You are a leader; everyone wants to follow you. Please take care to guide them in the right direction. You have a sense of adventure, taking care and cultivating God's creatures. You have a kind soul with a big heart who respects and cares deeply for the old and young. This I am most proud of. These words are only a small part of the deeper you and who you truly are.

I know it may not always seem like it, but I love you more than words could ever express. As a mother, I am here to guide you through the journey of becoming a man, by teaching you good morals, values, self-respect, and integrity. Sometimes life gets hard between a mother and a son. However, when you are older, you will understand that your joy is my joy and that your pain is my pain and that we both must stand strong against OCD and life's ups and downs. Just know I will always be here for you, during the good times and the bad, and you will always have a listening ear and a shoulder to lean on.

I am so proud of you and the young man that you have become. I am also proud to be your mother. I have been blessed beyond belief to have you in my life. You make me laugh, you make me cry, and you give me the best hugs. I cherish the times we spend together, and I love and anticipate seeing your face first thing every morning. You are an amazing son, brother, friend, and family member to so many! Continue your relationship with God and know and believe in your heart that all things are possible through Him.

And remember . . . Don't try to fit in! You were the one born to stand out. You are and will always be meant for big things in this world. Live your life to the fullest and never let anyone or anything deprive you of your happiness, my gorgeous boy.

I love you always!
Mom

Finding Hope Through Chelsea

Tricia Eisfelder

Dear Chelsea,

Gosh, where do I begin?

You were our "oops" baby, LOL! After seven years of having a family of four, we thought our family was complete. God had a different plan, though, because little did we know, it was far from complete.

You came into our lives five weeks early, which scared us to death, but everything turned out fine—you were just in a hurry to meet your new family. You brought love and laughter into our lives that we didn't even know were missing. Oh, I'm sure if you asked CJ and Josh at the time, they probably would have said a dog was a better idea. You very quickly wormed your way into their hearts, though, and they didn't know what hit them.

As the years went on, you grew up to be the little sister that followed them around and never gave them a moment to themselves, but they never complained. We soon started doing more things together and enjoying each other's company. You brought "family time" back into our lives. As you started middle school, you found the true meaning of "mean" girls, but you still tried to stay positive and continued on.

You loved baking as you got older and soon found that was the best way for you to release all the heartache/drama you were dealing with in school. Dad loved baking/cooking with you. Thank you for doing that with him. You gave him memories he'll hold onto forever.

High school and college weren't much different. You always struggled to fit in. I hated watching you go through that. When you started showing signs of depression and anxiety, we thought the best thing to do was talk to my doctor and start a medication that could help. CJ and I were already successfully taking meds for this. They worked for a while. You had the biggest heart and were so strong and brave, I thought there was nothing you couldn't get through.

Then you found Jesus, and your love for Him was contagious. Going to Christian concerts with you was so much fun. I thank God I have those memories. As time went on, though, life got harder and harder for you. I knew you struggled and at times had panic attacks. I tried hard to get you through them, but often felt lost in how to help. I think when you gained so much weight, you couldn't see the true beauty you had in you.

I'm sorry that you hurt so much. I wish there was more I could've done for you. I'll always wonder if I did all I could to help. I love you and I know deep down that leaving us isn't what you really wanted—you were just so tired. Please know we understand.

I hope I've made you proud with the Facebook page I started in your honor. Thank you for all the journal entries and snapshots of inspirational quotes you left me to put in it. Thanks to you, "Finding Hope Through Chelsea" will inspire and save lives! Thank you for being in our lives for as long as God allowed.

Walk those streets of gold, play cards, bake, do all the things you love. I can't wait to see you again one day. I loved you first and I'll love you forever.

Mom XOXO

For My Dearest Daughter

Victoria Powers

For my dearest daughter,

I can't imagine life without you. I was blessed to be the vessel for your existence in this world. We have fought through so much together that our bond is impenetrable. While in my womb at six months we went through open lung surgery. Three months later your beautiful self appeared weighing nine pounds and 21 inches.

From the very beginning, we were tightly bound together. We walked a parallel space doing everything together. We were never apart. Everyone thought we were the perfect mother and daughter. Such a pretty, friendly, outgoing baby girl. Such a sweet, adorable little girl. Pretty as a picture—but life isn't a picture.

School began and life took a difficult turn. Homework and the tedious hours of school were beyond your scope. School was a tremendous struggle, and no amount of extra help and tutoring eased the struggle or provided successful help. When high school approached, a dark cloud of depression took hold.

Our life changed with the death of your father and our move to a new state. The switch to a so-called "A+" Public High School did not prove to be effective. It was a nightmare for you, and it resulted in the school district dismissing you at 16 years old for medical reasons.

Further into the darkness we fell. Anxiety attacks and depression led to a hospitalization at 16. I had no tools to understand what was happening. The bright spot during that time was your artistic talent. You spent hours drawing by hand and on the computer. It was like a far-off light in a tunnel of darkness. We were trying to reach it, but it seemed so far away. Your artistic expression was this outstanding, haunting, raw talent. How brilliantly your pain and sadness shined in your art! What does a mother do with a depressed high school dropout with such raw, brilliant talent?

I wish I had the information and tools to understand what was happening. By age 21, a strange psychosis had started to take hold of you. I understood nothing, had no reference point or experience for the trauma and pain that we both lived in. Now, eight years later and four years medication compliant, we live in our new reality of schizoaffective bipolar disorder. We are learning to enjoy life while adapting to this brain disorder. On this journey, we will stumble and cry, but love is the powerful force that wills us to keep going forward and to keep fighting. My life purpose is to continue to learn and advocate for my loved one and for those who can't advocate for themselves.

Compassion Amid Chaos

Vikki Plessinger

I am a mother of two children with brain illnesses. One is trying so desperately to save his life. The other seems determined to end hers. My son has a very rare Central Neurocytoma tumor in the third ventricle of his brain with malignancy. And my daughter has a 17-year drug addiction that has led to psychosis.

We'll start with my son, my first-born baby. He had a fall and hit his head. His symptoms led to a CT scan which has led to eight months of appointments, scans, diagnoses, surgeries, and gamma knife radiation. He has lost cognitive abilities, memory, and, well, a lot of his life.

Justin,
This current journey of ours is so very difficult. The struggle of watching you fight . . . day after day . . . with determination to make this day better than the last . . . only to watch you get defeated at the end of the day.

But, watching you have one good day overcomes me with joy. I am so very proud of you. The love you share. Your morals and values. Your integrity. Your strength. I feel blessed that our relationship is so strong and close that I can share the struggles and triumphs with you. I love watching you interact with your loved ones, even on your worst days. I know it's so very hard for you.

You have somehow maintained your humor. I love when the doctors are confused and your response is, "I'm the one with the brain tumor, what's your excuse?" You make me smile.

It seems like an overwhelming fight with the finances, the insurance, the red tape, the conflicting thoughts from the doctors, the disability process, the trial and error on medications and procedures. Why does it have to be so difficult when you already have enough, too much, on your plate? It just seems like the establishments are doing their best to bring you down and set you up for failure.

But you strive on. We keep pushing. We are your village. We love you.

The unknowns of this tumor are scary. Will it spread? Will the radiation help or hinder your progress? Will your cognitive and memory issues resolve or will they get worse? Will you lose more functioning? How will we cope? How will we pay your bills? Will this take your life?

We will always be there for you, you know that. And we know that you don't want to have to depend on anyone for anything. You are an independent man and don't want help. But we all need help. We all do.

We wonder where God is. . . and yet we see His orchestration in everything. He's made it very clear that He's in this with us, and yet we still have questions. We remain steadfast that He knows what He's doing and it will all be for good. But we have to keep reminding ourselves of this. But for now, we will walk this journey one step at a time . . . together . . . with love.

Bralyn,
These last 17 years have been filled with worry, anxiety, fear, gut-wrenching pain, despair, anger, conflict, and tears—lots of tears. But they have also been filled with hope, determination, faith, understanding, compassion, patience, and always, love. Through these years, God has taught me many valuable lessons and initiated growth and maturity in me—sometimes against my will.

Yes, sometimes I had to learn and mature . . . or sink. The years of court systems, rehabs, and broken mental health systems. The years of defiance and secrets. The years of trying to pick up the pieces from your decline and trying to make things normal. The years of going all-in with your girls to try to show them a safe place, a constant. The years of waiting for "the call." And getting a few of them in the middle of the night . . . panicked when the doorbell rang, and a policeman was standing there. But relieved when I knew you were alive.

The years of not sleeping, of always anticipating the next bomb. Never fully being able to relax. I watched you when you couldn't speak or write a sentence that made sense. I watched you listen and talk to people I couldn't see. I watched you as you screamed and growled at the demons that had possessed you. I watched you spiral into this other world that I had no understanding of and no control over. I've watched you lose your faith.

Yes, I wanted to control this situation. I wanted to fix it. I fought. I fought when you wanted me to and I fought when you didn't want me to. I fought . . . I prayed. God, this is my daughter . . . help her!

But mixed in those years, I saw my little girl, scared, ashamed, confused, abused . . . hurting. I saw your immense pain. Wanting, needing, and seeking help, only to be let down by the system.

If the stars would just align where there would be help for you when you were ready. If only . . . I've watched you be an incredible mother. I've watched you enjoy family gatherings—bonfires, volleyball, swimming, vacations. I've watched you plan birthday parties, help the girls with schoolwork, teach them how to ride their bikes, play, and do crafts with them. I've watched you make individuals feel renewed by styling their hair and listening to them with compassion. Your compassion, your love, your caring, your interaction with others . . . I miss that. I miss you.

After three 72-hour holds that turned into 12 days in care, they were finally able to place you where you could get some help. I am very proud of what you have accomplished while at Cardinal. I am starting to see you again. And it makes me so very happy. It makes everyone happy. Jaylyn, Grace, your daddy, Karmen, Justin, Grandma Ruce, Aunt Tootie, the list is endless. You are so loved.

You will graduate from Cardinal before long. You have been clean and taking your meds for 44 days! That is a super-huge achievement. I am also scared... scared of losing you again. Afraid that the system will not provide the next step in your journey. Afraid it hasn't been long enough for you to stand tall, build confidence, work through all the demons in your life, and learn new healthy coping skills.

To Joseph, for His 32nd Birthday
Rebecca Reinig

Editor's Note: warning—suicide perspectives

If you or someone you know is thinking about suicide, please call 988 for the 988 Suicide and Crisis Lifeline or text the word HOME or START to 741741 for the Crisis Text Line.

Our youngest son, Joseph Reinig, would have turned 32 on July 3, 2023. He has been gone for 20 months now. I read people's stories and struggles with their loved ones suffering from mental illness, homelessness, and addiction, and my heart aches. Their story was our story. I totally understand and feel their pain.

Joseph was a kind, funny, compassionate young man. He touched people's lives everywhere he went. He loved everyone and everyone loved him. There were very few people that he did not like, and there was always a good reason—they were bad guys, as Joey would call them. We learned through the years that he was never wrong when he said that, and we stayed away from those people.

During the last few years of his life, Joe lived in transient camps in San Diego County. His delusions had him believing he could not live with us, or we would be killed. His life became a revolving door of jail, hospitals, rehab, and home.

At first, living in the camps worked for him. It was a tight-knit community of social outcasts who looked out for each other. As my son's disease progressed and his brain became more damaged, he could also be violent. As the time went on and his disease progressed, the people in the transient camps did not want him around because of his violent outbursts. He was eventually shunned from the camps and left to fend for himself. He truly existed in a living hell.

Although I would never wish death on anyone, my son's death was the best possible option for him. Now I know he is truly safe. I don't have to worry anymore, and I believe he is whole again. He left the shell of a body he occupied while on Earth, and he is dancing in the universe. I miss him every minute of every day. I miss the thought of what he could have been if the system had not failed him.

With that being said, I now understand that I wanted him to live for my own selfish reasons, my own happiness and peace. He always told us to let him die, that he was not meant to be on this Earth. I now believe he was right.

I no longer keep my phone nearby in case he calls. I no longer lose sleep worrying about him. I no longer live on the edge, waiting for the next crisis. I no longer wish he would just come home so we could love him up.

I believe that through our suffering there is always a lesson to learn. The lesson I have learned was the hard way, and now I have a clear understanding that sometimes love is just not enough to save someone. That was a hard lesson because I truly believed if we loved him unconditionally and never gave up, he would be okay. I did not realize that for him to be okay meant leaving this life on Earth. I miss him so much but understand he is now exactly where he was meant to be, and he is no longer suffering.

Rebecca Reinig writes, *"Joseph Reinig was the youngest son of our three boys. Joseph was raised in a happy, close, two-parent family. He died October 5, 2021. He died alone, in the bushes, in the rain. He took his life with a fentanyl overdose, only a few days after a two-week stay at a* *psychiatric hospital. He had admitted himself for suicidal ideations. He was dumped on the streets by the hospital staff, in spite of my pleas to hold him until I could arrive to pick him up. I waited for his call, to tell me where I could find him. That call never came. We will never know if his death was accidental or intentional. Either way, he knew the risks, and had lost his will to live."*

You Are Enough
Deborah Fabos

I've told you so many times that I love you and I've tried in every way to show you how much you mean to me. How proud I am of you. How I think you're so very handsome, funny, kind, and smart.

What I don't think I told you is how it broke my heart to see you suffer all those years when you were so very ill. Or that I would have gladly taken your place and set you free from psychosis if I could have. Oh, how I wished that so many times over the years.

I never told you how you saved me. How could I? How could I tell you that the changes I went through while loving you through this terrible brain illness that brought you so much suffering, saved me? It feels too selfish.

So I remain silent about this, although caring/advocating/loving you during your illness has made me a better person. How? Because I was a recipient of grace, mercy, compassion, and divine guidance for your sake—such wonderful gifts that I cherish. My soul would never have been touched by these gifts if it hadn't been for your pain.

I am deeply grateful, but I don't think I will tell you out of fear you will misunderstand my meaning. I would never want to cause you any more pain thinking I might actually be secretly happy that you have a brain illness. That's not what I'm saying.

What I'm trying to say is, since I couldn't take the brain illness from you, loving you through it, caring for your needs, and fighting for you have made me a better person. Maybe someday you'll be able to understand this.

I will tell you other truths. You are the best son I could ever hope for, and I am truly blessed to have you in my life. I love you with all my heart and soul. You are perfect, just as you are. I would go to hell and back again for you. I thank God for you.

You are enough.

Chapter 2. To the Parents

To Mom and Dad, With Love

David Meyers

Dear Mom and Dad,

The difficulties I have faced throughout so many years have been tumultuous and traumatizing. I'd like to think I have started to get through the worst of it, though maybe it shouldn't have taken this long. I have problems that still shine through even though I know so much of my soul has been restored.

So much of this happened in my own time. However, I appreciate how you have always lent a helping hand. I don't think anyone ever expected I would need quite so much help. I know growing up I read my stories to you often, and you were impressed. If somehow that emotional wherewithal could have been used in the midst of confusion and agony as a teenager, I'm sure I would have accomplished more than I have.

The truth of my cognitive difficulties is so much that I am not sure you could understand. They are truly disabling. You have seen my health deteriorate time after time again. Yet you have stayed resolved, never letting go. Despite this, I have needed to get proper help on my own time, as much as you'd like to think I don't need anything else.

My own resourcing has provided me with so many things I have now that I need. This includes my home, my grocery supply, my church, and my doctors. I think you can appreciate that I have done this. And that space that I have used to resource for myself can be used to be grateful for you.

In the course of recovery with my schizoaffective bipolar type illness and TBI, God wants to provide space for me to figure out things on my own. He also wants me to appreciate the doors you have opened. If I would have pushed through and tried to succeed normally with bipolar as a young man, it's hard to say what would have happened.

However, without filing for disability, things may have been much worse. You were caught in the crossfire and had no way of really knowing what to do. No kid comes with a handbook. On my end, I wanted no better than to make you happy, until my thoughts were too numerous and overwhelming. Then I took a few random steps to improve myself, but I think some of them hurt you.

I was just hoping to improve myself, and it often helped to do some guesswork. But I do think you know in a couple of cases my guesswork was wrong and I should have listened less to friends. I know in the past 15 years especially, things have changed a lot. I'd like to think I have a baseline I am expanding. At times of conflict, I lost sight of key elements of this, but maybe other aspects were intact.

I think you know by now recovery is not a straight line. God provides a shining light for me to find my own way. I want you to know I work on continual forgiveness and letting go. And I look forward to many good years to come.

Love,
David

An Apology and a Thank You

Katie R. Dale

Contributor's Note: Granted, this is a letter written in retrospect to my parents about my illness and what happened as it began. In writing this, I aim to show parents what it can be like when your child is going through an unexpected episode of bipolar and to show the priceless value of parental support through a child's struggle with mental illness.

Dear Mom and Dad,

Do you recall how depressed I was in 2003? It seemed like I was on the brink of the blackest bottoming out. Then, without notice, my mind was a buoy, bobbing on cresting waves of euphoria.

Evidently, the changes I went through my junior year of high school lent themselves to my breakdown. I guess the switch to private school wasn't all I expected it to be. I wanted a Christian education with a Biblical worldview, but it wasn't black and white that way. I was ignored by my classmates, sidelined for my poor soccer performance, shamed for being late or showing any opposition to the rules, and undermined when I began to have a voice.

My actions and behaviors may have been a bit strange, especially when I stalked my class crush, but I don't think I meant to embarrass him or you. I simply wanted everything to fall into place. After all, there's a place for everything, and a time for everything. I was just listening to my instincts...I think.

The days were trying. Mom, I remember you meeting my spiritual awakening with such a fear...even an unwanted denial. Dad, I felt as though you barely saw the depressed me. And then when I began to get happy again, Mom, you didn't know what to do. I'm sorry for jumping on the car and trying to call my classmate at 7:00 a.m. on a Saturday morning. Dad, I'm sorry I didn't know my spontaneous raps and rhymes were really a manic high. Though it was pretty cool I could do that, wasn't it?

I apologize for such crazy behaviors, but I understand that at the time none of us had a clue what I was going through. There was no one to brief us on the surprises that bipolar disorder would bring. Who would have known I was destined to break from reality and be disposed to this burden of a disease? It wasn't like there was a handbook that came with me at birth letting you know "at 16, Katie will quickly descend into bipolar depression and need immediate psychiatric care." There simply wasn't a sign or foretelling clue. At all.

So, not only do I apologize, but I thank you. I thank you for the patience you bore as my symptoms emerged. I thank you for getting me to a psychiatrist when you did. I thank you for your support and unwavering presence while I was in the hospital for 21 days. I thank you for your work to get me to an outpatient clinic for more help. I thank you for advocating for me at school, to keep me in classes so I could finish my studies to pass for the year. I thank you for your hearts of compassion, to see me at my worst and love me unconditionally. And I thank you for all the time and effort that went into keeping me well. You were my biggest supporters. I couldn't have made it out as well as I did without you.

To God be the glory. He was there in providing me the parents you have been to me. I hope this gives my story more clarity and closure for you. I love you.

Your daughter,
Katie

As a former psych ward patient and clinical case manager, **Katie Dale** *has unique first-hand experience with the mental healthcare system and the trials of serious mental illness from a faith-based perspective. She has documented her experiences in a memoir and in her online and in-person advocacy. Find her at KatieRDale.com and social media @katierdale.*

Letter of Redemption to My Mother
Cathy Bullock

Dear Claudia,

As I sit here anticipating the 2022 New Year and wondering what joys and sorrows it will bring, I remember you. Our world is in the midst of a deadly pandemic that frankly, I never thought I would experience in my lifetime. It's an experience akin to living in a sci-fi horror movie. I sometimes wonder if I could magically change the fact that you developed a serious mental illness when I was a child, if your brain had remained healthy and you were still alive, would you have been the kind of mother I could call and kvetch with about what a struggle the pandemic is for us all? However, you died seven years ago.

You were 74 years old when you died alone with both serious mental illness and dementia in an Atlanta-area nursing home. Even with dementia, you always remembered both me and Chris (your son, my brother). Your official cause of death was cited as some sort of multi-organ failure that came on suddenly. Personally, I think both the dementia and the multi-organ failure were a result of living with a poorly treated serious mental illness. I prefer the term "brain disease," because that is, in fact, what serious mental illness is; there is nothing "mental" about it. You were in horrible pain during the weeks leading up to your death, and Chris and I had to make terribly emotional decisions about hospice care and end-of-life treatment.

The last words you and I said to each other over the phone before you died were "I love you." I am beyond grateful those were our last words to each other. Our relationship had been rocky for a long time—since the onset of your untreated brain disease.

You were 16 years old when you gave birth to me in Atlanta. Being a pregnant, unmarried teen got you kicked out of school back then. You and Daddy did get married, but I know how ashamed you were of getting kicked out of school. Daddy was 17 years old, with conduct problems, could not read, and had already dropped out of school. After my birth, we lived with your parents, my grandparents, until I was five years old, and your parents bought you and Daddy your first small house.

You were 25 years old when I came home from elementary school with Mama Ruth (your mother, my grandmother) one October to find you sitting in the middle of the den floor sobbing and talking in a way that made no sense. You were supposed to take me to the school carnival along with your cousin. Mama Ruth couldn't figure out what was wrong with you and made me call your cousin and lie and say that you had the flu. I look back at that time as the "after time." The time after the disease which I call "the body snatcher" came for you. Yes, sadly, your illness seemed to me like something straight out of the old sci-fi movie called Invasion of the Body Snatchers. You looked the same, but your voice and behavior had dramatically altered.

During the "before time," the time before the body snatcher disease took you far away from me, I remember you as being so pretty, vivacious, and fun. I remember how beautifully you played the piano, teaching me how to swim at Clifton Springs, and playing rock and roll music on the record player while you taught me how to do the twist and limbo. You taught me to read before I went to elementary school and bought me books. You, Daddy, and I would go to The Varsity every Friday night and then y'all would go bowling with your league and take me along. I would always get to bowl with the yellow speckled ball.

But then the "the body snatcher" disease came for you. I was eight years old when it came that day that we were supposed to go to the carnival. You were never the same after that, except for brief periods of time. You still looked the same. Sort of. But your voice would change and become mean and scary, the look in your eyes would change, and even your piano playing would become angry and frenzied.

Your parents were ashamed of you after you got sick—Mama Ruth, especially. Your father called his sister, who was a nurse, and she recommended you go to the psychiatric hospital at Emory University. Mama Ruth would not agree. Daddy had begun staying away from home and working late. He seemed to have little to say about your illness, except that you were "crazy," and needed to be "put somewhere," but Mama Ruth would not allow it.

The result was that you suffered for years with untreated serious brain illness, and I grew more and more afraid of you—afraid of your delusions and violent outbursts. I would try to talk you out of your delusions, but of course that didn't work. I did learn that the TV needed to be turned off at times because of your delusions. I also learned that having friends over anymore was not a good idea. I learned to make sure my bedroom door stayed locked with my desk shoved in front of it when I am asleep. I learned to stay away from home as much as possible. The woods in the back of our house became my sanctuary.

Somewhere in the middle of your illness, a not-so-wise doctor told your parents and Daddy that having another baby might "cure" you. What the hell! So that is how Chris came to be born. Sometimes, you didn't even remember you had a baby, and I had to take care of Chris. I am ashamed to admit I resented my caretaking role at the time. I was nine years old when Chris was born. I am also ashamed to admit how afraid of you I was and how I couldn't wait to move out and as far away as I could manage.

Daddy and your parents did not understand your illness and weren't much help to you, either. You were hidden away at home. Sometimes you seemed to get better for periods of time, but those times never lasted.

I learned not to trust that "the body snatcher" had finally let you go. And it hadn't. I understand now that you were suffering from cycling in and out of mixed-manic episodes with psychosis, but at nine and ten years old, I had no idea.

Ultimately, decades later, your diagnosis fluctuated between severe bipolar disorder Type 1 with psychotic features and Schizoaffective Disorder, Bipolar Type. Your diagnosis of course depended on the doctor and how you presented yourself at the time.

At 12 years old, I started reading about mental illness. Life magazine had a huge article about schizophrenia, and I told my grandmother that I thought that's what you had. Finally, your parents took you to a psychiatrist! I still remember the medications you were given at that time: Tofranil, Stelazine, and Benadryl. Part of my job was to encourage you to take your medications, because you didn't want to. They made you gain a lot of weight, and they made you stiff. You began moving robotically, but I wasn't as afraid of you because they stopped your delusions. The problem was that you kept going off them. I did not know about anosognosia at the time, and so I blamed you for not wanting to be sane and healthy.

When I went away to college, I majored in psychology to try to learn more about your illness. I guess I had fantasies about not only saving you, but also getting my sparkling, fun mother back. Of course, there was limited understanding of brain illnesses back in the 70s and early 80s. Ultimately, I decided to become a special education teacher instead of a psychologist because, frankly, I always felt more comfortable working with children than with adults. Since Daddy couldn't read and you had gotten kicked out of school, I thought I could still make an important contribution on behalf of both of you as a special educator.

Knowing what I know now about brain disease, it was a psychiatrist you needed more than any other kind of professional and a psychiatric hospital. For years, as a young adult, I kept trying to find a way to get you into a hospital or a residential treatment facility in Atlanta. However, the normalization movement and deinstitutionalization made that impossible—unless you or I had been wealthy. The civil commitment laws in Georgia were also a challenge at the time. Hell, at one point in the early 90s right before I moved from Georgia to Iowa, I even learned about the new "miracle" drug that might help you. That drug was clozapine. I was unable to get you into a psychiatrist to prescribe it. Clozapine is now considered one of the gold standard treatments for your illness. I also found a lovely residential facility for adults with schizoaffective disorder and schizophrenia, but I couldn't afford it and you certainly couldn't. Daddy had divorced you when you were in your early 40s, so you no longer even had health insurance.

Eventually, as your untreated brain disease progressed, Chris and I began getting phone calls from Atlanta area police about you. Once you broke into a woman's home because she had left her door unlocked, and you decided you wanted somebody to bake you some cookies. When the terrified woman refused, you became belligerent and she called the police. Fortunately, the police were kind and knew Chris, so they called him and he got off work to come talk you into leaving the woman's home. She did not press charges against you.

For quite a few years, I limited my contact with you. I would apologize to you for that now, if I could. I guess I felt like I had to distance myself from you somewhat in order to survive myself. Still, that is not a good excuse. During that distance, I never stopped trying to find a way to get you proper treatment. I wish I could tell you that. How important it was for so long for me to try to find you appropriate treatment.

Claudia, I am so sorry that at one point you briefly ended up homeless. Chris and I were helpless to prevent that from happening; you would not take your medication. At another time in your senior years, you ended up in a nursing home that was shut down for a Medicaid fraud scandal that made the front page of the Atlanta Journal. I spent days on the phone trying to find a new nursing home for you. When I finally found one with an available bed, it's because I happened to call at a time when a patient had recently died and so a bed had just opened up. That nursing home treated you well, I think. It was a depressing place, but it was adequate. It was the best I could find given the financial constraints and your needs. You made friends with another patient there for a while, and the staff seemed to like you. The medications the new nursing home put you on were Depakote and Quetiapine. Those two medications seemed to work well for you for a long while, but the problem was by the time you got access to them you had developed dementia.

At one point, you quit walking. Chris and I could never figure out why. The nursing home staff had no answer, except that you had become unsteady and they thought you may have developed Parkinson's disease on top of the severe bipolar/schizoaffective disorder and dementia. I have since learned that if psychotic disorders go untreated for a long time, or are improperly treated, brain damage can occur. I believe that is what happened in your case, Claudia. I am so sorry that happened to you. So very sorry.

Because you developed a serious brain disease in the 1960s, you suffered for 49 years from a lack of appropriate treatment and misunderstanding from your own family. Your life was devastatingly tragic. Even now, with the current knowledge I have, it is hard for me to comprehend why you would not take your medication. Of course, I know the answer is anosognosia. I completely understand your refusal on an intellectual level, but on an emotional level I still struggle. I struggle with wanting to turn back time and somehow change things so that you could access proper medication and proper treatment. I also can't help but wonder how much of a role shame and discrimination played in your suffering. I have found some advocate friends I wish you could meet. Advocating and working to promote understanding of serious brain illness to the degree possible is the best I can do for you, now.

I do want you to know that I will be forever grateful that your last words to me and my last words to you were, "I love you." And I did. I do.

Love,
Cathy, your daughter

Dr. Cathy Bullock *is a veteran special educator and advocate for individuals with serious mental illness. Her advocacy work includes serving on the policy committee of the National Shattering Silence Coalition (NSSC) and teaching about mental illness when given the opportunity.*

Dearest Dad

Helen

It has been 20 years since you took your own life. I have only just begun to openly talk about your life and death. Why? Maybe it was because we didn't celebrate your life with family and friends in early February 2001. Maybe it was because I didn't fully understand the extent of your mental illness. Maybe it was because you and Mom moved to Florida in 1972 and there wasn't much visitation between the families.

Thanks for being my father. I am blessed to call you "Dad" and want to tell the world about our life together.

I remember living in our small house when I was very young. I was unaware that most six-year-olds didn't go to bed while the sun was still shining brightly. Mother would fix supper for Nancy and me. She would not eat with us but ate with you when you came home from work. She told us that you liked "things" quiet in the evening.

Moving into Nana's two-story house in 1952 was a little different, since the sisters lived upstairs. We were preteens and delighted to have our own phone upstairs. Our bedroom happened to be above your bedroom. We had to be "quiet" when we went to bed since you had "trouble going to sleep." When I think back to my teen dating days, I thought it was weird that my curfew was either before 11 p.m. or after midnight. Again, Mother explained that you had "trouble going to sleep."

You always had a garden in which you worked on weekends or the evenings when we were older. Nancy and I loved working in the garden with you. It was "our time" alone with you. The garden hoe was your favorite tool. Little did I realize this was the beginning of what I assume now was OCD. You wanted everything organized and the garden to be perfect with no weeds.

But, oh boy, did we have lots of fun on our vacations together! We went to General Butler State Park for our first two vacations. I remember sitting on the cabin porch overlooking the lake. That is where the sisters learned to play gin rummy, where we watched thunderstorms come across the lake, and where we ate family meals together.

You must have earned more vacation time in 1955, since this was the beginning of our vacations to Daytona Beach. We spent two weeks vacationing in a small cottage on the quiet beachfront. In 1960, the Florida beach vacation became three weeks. It was a great family time playing in the surf, walking the beach, and just sitting quietly on the beach towels.

Taking our yearly trips to Florida was the beginning of my love of maps and all things geographic. This was the time before the country was covered with interstate highways. You and I carefully mapped our trips to Florida and back each summer. We always went a different way. We wandered all over Tennessee, Alabama, and Georgia visiting new towns and tourist attractions.

When you retired to Florida in 1972, I struggled with the fact that you didn't want to visit Kentucky for more than a few days at a time with my family. The kids were bursting with joy when we spent a week at Christmas time with you and Mom. While we were there, you spent a lot of time taking long walks by yourself. I never thought to talk with Mom and ask any questions. I just assumed that your exercise preference was walking.

I was most upset with you when Mother had her open-heart surgery in late August 1988. You didn't want Nancy or me to come to Ocala. You simply told us that you "were okay and could handle things by yourself." Your other excuse was that Nancy and I were both teaching at the time. Well, I'm very glad that I turned the tables on you during that Labor Day weekend. I called your pastor and told him that I was flying to Florida without your knowledge. We worked out a plan and your church friends picked me up at the airport. I can still remember the gigantic hug when you opened the door. And, yes, there were tears. You were, indeed, glad to see family, and Mother's recovery improved so much in those few days.

When Mother died with ovarian cancer in 1999, her surgery was on a Monday. Again, you didn't want the sisters to come to Ocala. One of my saddest moments was your phone call telling me that her tumor was so large that it was useless to remove. You still didn't want us to come visit at that exact moment. The plan was to visit in ten more days which would be Memorial Day weekend. The very last time that I was able to talk to Mother coherently on the hospital phone was Thursday.

Your call the next day informed us that she had been moved to a Hospice House. She was gone within 40 hours. We visited over Memorial Day weekend and stayed a few more days so we could bring her ashes home with us. There was a private family burial without you. "I've already told her good-bye" was the only thing you told Nancy and me as we walked out your door.

Thank you again for being my father. I will cherish all these memories as I begin to think about your life and share the stories with my family and friends.

Most lovingly,
Helen

With Love and Faith from Jonny Cakes

Jonna Terhune

Letter to my best friend. I call you Mom.

I never thought I would make it this far. You stood by me through all the sleepless nights, not just as an infant, but as a teenager and adult when mania engulfed me, or depression strangled my heart and mind. How many times did you sit in the hospital wringing your hands and whispering a prayer of safety and love to God for saving my life? Your faith in a future where I could love God as much as He loves me never wavered. I'd beg for you to let me go but letting me go never entered your mind.

You are a strong and loving mother that may not have always known what to do, but you managed to do just what was called for. I fought these tremendous battles, but I never fought them alone. You have always supported me to become who I was meant to be even when we weren't sure exactly who that was. I haven't been able to express my gratitude to you for everything you've done and continue to do. I pray that I can continue to make you proud as I become a better version of myself.

I started out with this brain disorder as a frightened and rebellious 15-year-old. For some time, we all thought that I might be living in a state hospital riddled with delusions for an indeterminate amount of time. As you encouraged a life of recovery and stability, I slowly managed this disorder and I no longer identified as a bipolar disordered person. I became the woman who lived with a diagnosis and succeeded. I am so proud to be your daughter, a survivor, and a child of God.

Thank you for all you do and all you have done

.

With love and faith,
Jonny Cakes

Jonna Terhune writes, *"I am a social worker living with a diagnosis of bipolar disorder, but it does not define me. By the grace of God, I am still alive and blessed to have the support of my best friend/mother. I know this letter cannot show the extent of sacrifice and love that my mother has given to help me live, but I do hope that it gives a glimpse into our experience. I pray that one day I can give back as well as pay it forward."*

Dear Mom and Dad

Jill Crawford

Dear Mom and Dad,

Thank you for loving my battered soul and caring for me when all I could do was hurt and hate myself. Thank you for the care and support. The hours of holding my hand through what we later learned were panic attacks. Thank you for taking me to the ER, as numerous doctors tried to find the cause of my unease. My disease, which we later learned was called manic depression, or bipolar when we went to a psychiatrist. Dad, thank you for the many overtime hours you worked so our family could have a stay-at-home mom and healthcare. Thank you, mom, for being my angel. Thank you for always offering the hope that life can get better and that I could be well. I now live a happy, healthy life in marriage with a family of my own because of your steadfast love and care. Thank you.

From Mom

Oh, Jill, what a beautiful letter you wrote. You know Dad and I are proud of the person you have become. But remember, you did the hard work to make all this happen! We love you so much. Mom.

From Dad

Thank you, Jill. We did what we thought was the right thing to do for our children. As you have now learned as a parent, each child is different, and their needs are different. You do what you can and hope it is good enough. Raising a child with a medical condition that is not yet recognized by the medical community is tough. It is not just hard to get the right medicine to help, it was hard to get any medication to help. Thankfully they now understand what bipolar is and how to treat it.

Love,
Dad

Letter to My Parents

Jay Tapscott, CPS, BA

Dear Mom and Dad,

I love you dearly, and do not fault you with regards to the why of my mental health condition. However, you were not really emotionally available for me or my brother. I did not realize that until recently when my younger brother gave voice to that fact. You struggled and had trouble helping me and my brother learn to regulate or co-regulate, and therefore to self-regulate, partially because of your parents' parenting. It is a vicious cycle that I am attempting to break. I had to learn to regulate for myself later and unlearn the habits of not regulating myself.

Thank you for having a hand in breaking me, Mom and Dad. Thank you for breaking me wide open so I could be molded into fertile soil for seeds of wisdom and hope to take root in me—so that I could grow into a mustard tree and sow hope-filled seeds for others. As a practicing, faith-filled Christian, I feel like I am constantly swimming upstream, constantly fighting for what I believe to be right.

The other day at work I shared that one of my mantras to help me regulate and to overcome intrusive thoughts that are the result of childhood trauma was "God is good." The response I got back from a person that I have the privilege of serving was them asking me if I was kidding. I had to fight off shame and let them know that I was serious. God is my rock, my hope, and my salvation. You, my parents, instilled this faith in me and I am eternally grateful.

In this country, there are a couple of different types of people and a couple of different types of Christians. Dad, you rail against the "evangelicals" (you say that word with a contemptuous sneer) that only believe in one miracle, the resurrection. Recently, I was at a Lenten church service. The shared reading from the Bible was the Old

Testament story of Noah, his family, and the flood. The preacher gave a caveat and said that this story never actually happened, although there is fossil evidence that there was a flood. Maybe it did not cover the entire world, but for that culture, it covered the known world. Also, there are other older religions and traditions that also have a flood story, so it makes me wonder if you are correct, Dad.

That kind of fundamentalism is putting Christ and Christianity in a bad light and stealing hope from many people who are otherwise on the fence. Many Christians really are blind to science's breakthroughs. I speak now of the vaccines and other medical advances that many Christians sneer at and say, "I don't need that; I have the Holy Spirit." There is a middle ground. You taught me that, with your emphasis on inclusion and tolerance, with your introducing me to other religions which have their own intrinsic value. You taught me that it is possible to believe in the message of Christ and the way it offers as love, and to also be a modern American in the world, and to hold on to hope during that process of discovery. You guys, Mom and Dad, have taught me that even as I struggle with my mental health issues.

For us to heal and to have real hope, we as a family, a society, a culture, and nation have to learn to reward spontaneity and vulnerability—something you guys should have but did not do for me—and to be nonjudgmental and non-shaming. We need to learn to regulate as a national culture so we can conquer these endemic issues that plague us. We as a country are a world leader. Mom and dad, you guys taught me to see the bigger picture. I believe that if we learn to regulate as a nation, it can be contagious and we can bring hope to the entire world, but it has to start with acceptance and forgiveness at the family level, especially regarding mental health and self-care.

To do that, we have to surrender to the community. That is one of the keys of self-regulating, trusting others, letting down our guards, being vulnerable.

Self-care and regulation on a global level could be a game changer to bring hope and make it a reality. I believe we need to broaden our view to include all humans, not just the ones that are like us, not just the ones in our family, or that we intrinsically like or understand, because there is more alike between us than different. My parents taught me that too.

The hope for our future lies within how globally inclusive we become as a species. All war is infighting, whether we like it or not. Christianity says love your neighbor. This needs to be an international undertaking so that becomes a reality. Otherwise, there is no hope. We have reached a crossroads combined with a bottleneck. We are in the midst of a time of change for our civilization, for humanity. We need to make the hard choices and sacrifices now, or we will not make it.

For the balance to tilt into hope rather than despair, now is the time to lean into community and broaden our view of what that could mean. You, my parents, have taught me, even as much as you have broken me open to be fertile soil, to be inclusive and accepting. I never wondered whether you loved me, even as I realized that you were not given the tools to properly raise me, as disturbed as I was growing up. That is a tough ask, and you did your best, and I love you for it. Thanks, Mom and Dad! Your sacrifices have not been in vain. I hope you're proud of my philosophical viewpoints, which you helped to engender in me, that I hope to share with the world each day that I have breath.

Love,
Jason

Jay Tapscott, *CPS, BA is a poet, author, and also a Peer Specialist dealing with schizoaffective disorder and working in an inpatient psychiatric unit where he was once a patient in Philadelphia. There, he models wellness as he visibly coexists with his psychiatric condition in that setting, seeking to offer hope and encouragement by doing so.*

Clean for Over a Year
Michelle B.

Dear Mom,

I'm writing you this letter to tell you how much you mean to me. You have been there for me and for that I am grateful. As you know, I have been clean for over a year now. I want to express how deeply sorry I am for disappointing you with my drug use.

You always tried to help me with my mental health even when I was young. I never listened and would suffer. You saw the outbursts, the psych wards, and the meltdowns. I felt them. I self-medicated through meth use. It was like magic. Now I know this not to be true.

After going to a psych doctor and getting diagnosed with bipolar and anxiety, I take medication. It helps balance me out. The abuse I've gone through with different men has caused depression along with my mental health issues. It was always hard to tell you I was using drugs. You and the boys just thought I was crazy. But it was domestic violence, meth use, and being bipolar all in one.

You always stuck up for me when people called me crazy. I just want to thank you for sticking by me and recognizing I had mental health issues and wasn't crazy. Through therapy, medication, and being off drugs I've seen my life improve. Thank you for taking care of my precious children. I will soon have my baby girl in my custody. I love you for caring for her.

Staying sane takes work. Accepting my mental health is ongoing. Thank you for always being aware of my bipolar and supporting treatment. I love you, mom.

Love,
Your daughter, Michelle

When Mental Illness Disrupts Your Life
From Holding to Hope
By Brad and Donna Hoefs

In 1975, my life, as well as the lives of my entire family, was disrupted, interrupted and changed forever. What happened? Well, my father had a nervous breakdown (that's what it was called back then). He had his first episode of depression with his bipolar disorder. ~Brad

At the time, we didn't know it. This was a strong, almost "thuggish" man with a bad temper but who could also be a lot of fun. He was busy adding on to our house and doing all kinds of things with farming and feeding the cattle, and all of a sudden, he became a puddle of tears. It was shocking. I didn't know how to respond to it at all. I was a senior in high school. I was busy living, having a good life, and my father became very withdrawn, wasn't doing anything, and was crying a lot. It was very hush-hush even within our immediate family, and heaven forbid we would talk about it with anybody else. Finally, they got him to a doctor, a psychiatrist who diagnosed him right away and put him on lithium. This disruption took a while, and it was painful. And I remember it yet to this day . . .

Prayer:

Father . . . forgive me for putting blame on my loved one for their behavior, as if they can willingly control the chemistry of their brain. Keep me mindful that they are just as upset with this "disruption." Give me the mind of Christ, that I may be compassionate, empathetic, and wise. Most of all, please grant me the ability to be encouraging and supportive as we travel this journey together.
In Jesus' name. Amen.

Brad Hoefs *is the founder of Fresh Hope for Mental Health, and today is the full-time Executive Director.* **Donna Hoefs** *is a facilitator for Fresh Hope's Trauma Healing groups. The Hoefs are ever so grateful for the Lord's redemptive work in their lives. They are living proof that there is always hope!*

Chapter 3. To the Partners

Living Our Wedding Vows

Janet Coburn

The man I married didn't know I had bipolar disorder. To be fair, I didn't know either. I was famously moody and given to what would now be called major depressive episodes. Despite having had mostly a long-distance relationship, you and I took our vows.

You had studied psychology and worked as an aide in a psychiatric facility (no, that's not where we met). We seemed the perfect, if dysfunctional, couple. But I maintain that all couples—and all families—are dysfunctional in some way, at some level.

Naturally, you and I had our disagreements. One of the first surfaced when you tried to "shrink" me, figure out all my problems and help me overcome them. It annoyed me greatly: You weren't qualified to do that, and if I wanted a shrink, I would have hired one.

Next you tried humor to pull me out of my depressive fogs. That didn't work either. When I'm that depressed, humor can't get through. I think you finally realized that when you told me a joke and I didn't laugh. Then you told the same joke again and I still didn't laugh. Depression was no longer something for you to study, but to live with.

A number of years later, I entered a major depressive episode. I lost my job and was unable to work. I was unable to take care of myself, or the house, or the pets. The only things I could do were sleep and cry. You took up the slack. You were often frustrated or angry that I wasn't getting any better. Still, you took over all the caring duties, one after the other.

At last, I did start seeing a psychiatrist and received my proper diagnosis of bipolar 2 disorder with anxiety. The diagnosis cleared up a lot of things that had been happening, and once I was on medication, the symptoms seemed to ease—but they didn't go away.

My psychiatrist and I went through drug after drug. My therapist and I worked through symptom after symptom. The baseline when I started was that I called myself "pathetic."

We tried couples counseling, but it didn't seem to help. Once you and I went to a couples counselor through your EAP and the woman absolutely shredded me. Why wasn't I able to help you around the house? Why couldn't I give you more support? I wanted to yell, "Hello? Treatment-resistant bipolar disorder! I think I could carry a few books up the stairs, but Dan would have to sort them and put them away."

About this time, you experienced some depression of your own. You suffered for several weeks—maybe a month. I felt you were beginning to understand what I was going through. "Just imagine that this feeling lasted for several months, even several years," I said. "What would you do then?"

"I don't know," you replied. "I couldn't handle it."

"Welcome to my world."

After three years of unremitting depression, it started to lift. I decided to both get a job and go back to grad school. This may have been my hypomania talking, but there I was, working third shift and trying to teach and study immediately thereafter. Again, you took up the slack. If I was too tired to drive myself to the university, you took me there and picked me up afterwards. You even thought of a way to help me with my many papers. You took my reference books, went through the index looking for names and keywords, then flagged them with Post-It notes as I wrote.

When I have been in the depressive phase, you have worked to make things easier for me —doing the cooking; finding me clean towels (and even reminding me when I need to bathe); running errands, including picking up my medications; encouraging me and even going with me when there is something I absolutely have to do, like apply for disability; helping me think up topics for my weekly blog posts; keeping the house running and the pantry full—all the things you think a spouse might do for someone who is physically disabled. But I am, at many times, mentally disabled.

There have been bright spots, when my disorder recedes a bit. You and I have traveled some (though even then, depression has sometimes hit me unexpectedly), from local trips to ones overseas. I have learned to laugh at your antics. Now that I am better controlled on medication, our life is much closer to "normal." I am able to work part-time from home and bring in money. I pay the bills and do anything else that can be accomplished by computer. Yet you still surprise me with my favorite meals and snacks, help me when I need it, and constantly shower me with love and affection—kissing me on my head; stroking my hair till I fall asleep; holding me in your safe, warm arms.

Next year, we will have been married for 42 years. I can't say they've all been wonderful, because they haven't been. You and I fight like any married couple, and my disorder has made it difficult for us to have a "normal" life.

But if there's one thing I've learned from all this, it is that you are a true and precious caregiver. You took a vow to love me "in sickness and in health" and you have surely been fulfilling it ever since.

Janet Coburn *lives in Ohio with her husband of 41 years, Dan Reily. She also lives with bipolar 2 disorder. A graduate of Cornell University and the University of Dayton, Janet writes two blogs, bipolarme.blog and butidigress.blog, which she posts in every Sunday. She often contributes articles on mental health to* The Mighty *website. Janet has also written two books on bipolar disorder,* Bipolar Me *and* Bipolar Us.

Letter to Greg, My Lover

Diane Mintz

Lover, our life together has been like no other, and we went through fires before we even met. We have had many challenges yet so many victories and blessings along the way.

I thought that I finally had a grasp on our mental health conditions back in 2013, since it took me seven years of observing our recovery road to write our story "In Sickness and in Mental Health: Living With and Loving Someone with Mental Illness." Since then, there have been many twists and turns revealing even more around each bend. We had no idea that rougher terrain was yet to come.

We certainly have had a marriage of multiple miracles. The fact that I have not had an extreme manic or depressive episode with a bipolar 1 diagnosis since 1991—throughout the incredible challenges we have faced—blows my mind. God always had bigger plans for us than to just survive. He opened doors for me to speak openly to many audiences from students to law enforcement, free many silent sufferers of mental illness, and stop stigma. Thank you for allowing me to share and follow the mission I felt I was called to do, because just that drop in the ocean made ripples and waves like only God can do.

The past three years have been the biggest challenge in our marriage. We did not anticipate that you would be on your back 95% of the time and need to undergo several procedures and two radical spine surgeries, all while battling our invisible foe: your brain...and mine.

I believe that your complex diagnosis of dissociative identity disorder (DID) might have saved you from feeling the constant intensity of physical pain all these years, but the mental struggle was another layer of pain that was unbearable for you and left me feeling helpless, confused, and distraught. I couldn't understand why the pain was so intense you couldn't stand up, yet other times the pain seemed far away. Now I know that when your amazing brain split into parts to protect you from what a child's brain cannot deal with on its own, it sensed physical pain in parts as well. Before the MRI that showed the pain that was always there, I didn't understand what you felt was always different and why I felt insane trying to figure it out!

DID still remains a mystery to me despite knowing "about" your diagnosis. I still can't wrap my mind around your internal struggle when I see you from the outside managing our business and loving me and the kids through it all without letting on what goes on inside.

I marvel at your brilliant brain. You have a perfect recall of every client's computer network that you set up. You can simply "see" how to build, create, and remodel our homes. What a gift! Yes, you have a terrible thorn in your side to suffer the mental anguish you do, which was made even worse in times of physical pain, but you persevered! You are my hero.

Clearly, I have made many mistakes by reacting badly and taking things personally when I really needed to be quiet. Even if I can't recognize your dissociative states, I should always empathize with the pain that caused them. The thought of you as a child living in such a volatile, rageful environment that your mind had to escape into alters to handle it for you, breaks my heart and won't allow my mind to fathom!

I realize as I am writing this that I built a wall around my empath heart with only you, to protect me from feeling all of your pain. It has hurt us and I am trying to tear it down and be healthy enough to have boundaries, not walls.

Sadly, very few people talk about their experience with what was once called "multiple personalities" to make it comfortable for you to talk about. I get that! I was a pioneer in our world when I opened up about having bipolar disorder only a decade ago! It is awful to think you are alone and judged. I think Hollywood has done great damage in portraying DID, leaving the victims of abuse to suffer in silence still. Yet the biggest obstacle is that many psychiatrists don't believe in it at all, which made it hard for me to believe for a long time. I am so sorry for my unbelief.

I do believe there are far more people with DID than the estimated 1.5% that is reported. Tragically, there is a lot of childhood trauma. Neither of us understood what was going on with you for many years, so I believe it is still a hidden disorder for many. We know three other people with this diagnosis just in our circle of friends.

Our love and faith kept us together but if it wasn't for your courage and perseverance, you wouldn't have survived. I nearly lost my mind trying to "help" you with the list of temporary remedies and words of encouragement when I had none left to give. I often forgot it wasn't up to me, but the One who brought us together, and He is faithful always.

This year, God blessed us with the miracle of the spine fusion that allowed you to walk again. What a game changer to allow you to go back to the projects you love and let your brilliant brain spring back into action—the miracle of miracles!

Clearly, our story has many more chapters for me to write. I will start on the second edition with Part 3 this year. We have only scratched the surface to our understanding of DID, but I am committed to learning and adapting. When I think of how rare it is to find a therapist with DID expertise and you found one, I am certain we are on another of God's amazing missions. I am so blessed to be on it with you.

Diane Mintz

Author Speaker Advocate she/her/hers

Consumer Family Member Reviewer, Behavioral Health Concepts

Cell: 916-549-1755

An Answered Prayer

Craig Willers

My love letter is to the girl who actually loves me!

Her name is Mindy, and I distinctly remember praying to God in my misery for a girl who would love me. Here's our story.

We met on a blind double date singing karaoke. Her friend asked me out and made the mistake of bringing Mindy. I fell right away but didn't know if our feelings were mutual. She looked like Taylor Dayne, and it was in 1989 so that was the style. I fell for her looks and as we got to know each other, I fell for her loving and beautiful heart.

Three days of dating and I knew it was serious, so I had to tell her my secret. I told her I was a Paranoid Schizophrenic and that if she wanted to end it then, I would understand. She thought for a moment and then said, "Okay." Three years later we married, and it's been 30 years now.

We've been through so much, yet we're still the mushy 20-somethings who fell in love.

Thank you, Mindy, for loving me and for being my answer to prayer. I love you.

My Dear Craig
Mindy Willers

My Dear Craig,

I remember the night we met. Mea called and said I *had* to go with her. She had asked this guy out and couldn't go alone. I wasn't in the mood but agreed. Picked her up and drove to the karaoke bar. Then I saw you. You brought your friend like Mea brought me. I wasn't interested at first but then you started singing and I fell. But I felt bad because Mea asked you out. We continued to sing, closing the bar down, then went to your grandparents', where you were living. We immediately hit it off—found out we had a lot of things in common. I went home around 4 a.m. She stayed and you guys talked more. She called me later that morning and I apologized to her, but she was fine.

We met up later and you cooked moldy French toast—LOL. You told me then you had schizophrenia, and for some reason it didn't faze me. Went home. Talked to my mom. No concern indicated there. Did my research. That was 34 years ago. We've been married for over 30 years. There have been ups and downs, but God has been with us every step. I'm so proud of how far you've come and what you've done. I'm glad I went that night. I love you more every year, and I'm thankful you stuck with me too. You take care of me and treat me like a queen. I'm so spoiled. I love my baby more and more each year. Thank you for loving me back.

What a Ride It Has Been
Caroline Lehman

What a ride it has been! When we fell in love in high school, I had no idea what our future was going to look like; I just knew I wanted to be by your side. By the grace of God, we have been together for more than 25 years. At the time you had your first psychotic episode, I was worried about our future. What did mental illness look like? What did it mean for our little family? We definitely had some hard years, but through it all, you fought so hard to get better.

The word bipolar is scary, but you have proved that it can be managed with the help of doctors, medicine, self-care, community, and Jesus. Through all these years of challenges, fighting for you has always been worth it. You are smart and funny and witty and creative, the most self-aware person I have ever met, and you invest so much time and energy into our family.

You are consistently looking for ways to help each of us grow and be our best selves. You are wise beyond your years, willing to continue to do the hard work to make your disease manageable, and eager to help others in their journey with their mental illness.

I love you and am proud to be your wife!

Love,
Caroline

Love Letter to Sweet C from Ray

Anonymous

I am not proud of the symptoms of my bipolar and how they have affected my life and you and our children. I am saddened by the angry outbursts, sudden but lasting irritability, the delusional paranoia, and long bouts of extreme fatigue and depression that left me feeling useless in many ways. I appreciate you and how you handled everything when your world was also crashing down around you and I was in the psych ward, leaving you wondering what kind of life lay ahead of you. Your strength and your caregiving were and are amazing.

It is in this time of recovery as defined by mental health I have reached a place that I, at many times, did not think was possible. This was through extensive therapy, medication, routine, and meaning given by God. But currently, it is being in a good place that creates new obstacles and new challenges in our family. It may seem like we are fighting for control, but it is the fact that you have been in a lengthy role of caretaker, trusting in my decision making now becomes more difficult. The past has hindered you from allowing me to become more of a partner in the decisions. I am longing for and need your help in re-establishing more of my role as husband and father in the family.

We are learning anew how we are to relate to one another now that my self-medicating, addictive behaviors have been surpassed and the depressive fatigue of sleeping up to 16 hours a day are finally in the past. I desire more of the respect a man longs for and requires in order to be loving to their significant other, as we have found in the book *Love and Respect.*

This ride has been a wild one, but our commitment to one another has never ceased, and the good times have been really good and worth fighting for. When we are on the same page, we are an unbeatable team.

I will always love you, but when I have a hard time liking you, I will choose to work towards being in love again and again because it is important to me that we don't just stay married but that we have a marriage that is transparent, vulnerable, passionate, and meaningful.

I love you, my Sweet C, and I love the life we are currently living and providing for our kids. It may not be material in nature, but the things we have in our family—love, fun, God, community, and knowledge of how to live our best life—make this time in our marriage so exciting and rewarding. Thanks for saying yes to us nearly 25 years ago and every day since.

Love,
Ray

Dear Jen
Eric Riddle

Dear Jen,

It's not very often that I write a love letter to you while acknowledging that it may be published one day. So, in light of that reality, I endeavor to write an intimate letter to you that gives other potential readers a window into the role of my mental health diagnosis in our relationship.

I will never forget that when we met, one of the first things that you said to me was that you studied behavioral psychology. As you know, I was dating someone else at that time, so our conversations were with only platonic intent. However, looking back, I can confidently say, "You had me at behavioral psychology."

No matter how well I am feeling or for how long I have been symptom-free, I live with a history of hours of talk therapy, four hospitalizations, daily medicine for over half of my life, and memories of many moments merged with a mood disorder. You have only known me as someone with a diagnosis and yet you completely embrace all of me.

Thankfully, for over ten years since we married, my mental health has been strong. The last nine years since my last hospitalization have been the most stable years of adulthood. I know that our relationship is the most important protective factor in maintaining balance. Thank you. Your practical nature, linear mental processing, compassionate character, and discerning disposition have all helped steady me when I am edging towards overwrought, negative self-talk or unrealistic, energetic ideation. When I am getting lost in complex thoughts or emotions, you help guide me out with well-grounded advice.

You have fulfilled my prayer that began after my divorce to find a woman who loved Jesus, loved children, and had an incredibly joyful smile.

Seeing you at church with the kids on Sunday mornings, smiling as they gather to hear you share your love for Christ, reminds me of how blessed I am to have married you. You do not dumb down your theological inspirations for the children, but rather challenge them and share your own stories of the mysteries of faith. In doing so, you also help me seek to strengthen my own faith and find peace during troubling times.

After getting back from our wonderful 10th anniversary trip a few months ago, I've been going through one of the more difficult emotional periods since we married. While we both realize that much of the distress is focused on my work situation, the self-doubt and anxiety that have been dredged up during this time hold space in our relationship. I admit to being afraid that I will sink into a long-term depression like I've experienced in the past. I'm thankful that we've been able to talk through these feelings rather than ignore the fact that they are bubbling up.

The fear of uncontrollable emotional gloom is no stranger to me. However, it occurs to me that we can welcome those feelings into our household for a time. Rather than shutting the door and trying to force them away, we can allow those feelings to sit with us, and we can learn from them. I think that with that sense of fearless hospitality, we can open our hearts to the presence of pain and have faith that even those feelings can become a sort of friend. Probably not the kind we want to invite to every festivity, but one that challenges us with the wisdom of pathos. I'm confident that these times serve as a means of life calibration, developing stronger faith, and experiencing unexpected growth. With you by my side, it has before and will again.

Today, I revisited the Revealing Voices podcast question, "What does healing mean to you?" I remembered that my recorded response was about being restored to community. Much of my personal healing happened when you encouraged people from our church to visit me at the hospital back in 2013. With mental health stays, most families' reactions are to keep it a secret. In our first real encounter with my mental illness as a married couple, you sought to understand the situation and trusted your instinct to invite people to join me. Thank you for nudging me towards sharing my struggles with mental illness. In doing so, it has been one of the most healing aspects of my recovery—I can point to that time as my first conscious, dedicated work toward restoration into community.

I'm honored that you chose me to be your husband. When I think about the fact that you knew I had a diagnosis before we met, it astounds me that you leaned into our relationship and continued to pursue me, even when I stepped away. I'm dedicated to being the healthiest that I can be, knowing that focusing on our relationship is always at the heart of restoration. Sometimes you accept me before I can accept myself—and because of that, it has helped me gain confidence regardless of how I feel. I am thankful that I chose you to be my wife.

I have always thought there is something about the behavioral psychologist background in you that marvels at my random thoughts, unexpected passions, creative impulses, and occasional vibrant energy. Perhaps these are some of the benefits of bipolar disorder.

Thank you for riding the ups and downs and, when the ride gets a little wild, holding on to me and having fun amidst the turbulence. With my idiosyncrasies—some intentional and others seemingly at the whim of my emotions, I'm glad that I can make you happy with that joyful smile of yours! You may never quite figure me out, but I know you'll always bring your care, wisdom, and curiosity to strengthen our relationship.

It is with an abundance of gratitude that I share this life journey with you and know that unconditional love will overcome all—including a mental health condition!

Sincerely,

Eric Riddle

Eric Riddle *co-founded the* Revealing Voices *podcast with Tony Roberts in 2018 and remains a contributor through the monthly* Haikast *podcast series. Eric works full time as a Development Coordinator for Faith in Place, an interfaith environmental and racial justice nonprofit. He traces his love for environmental work to mission work in 2006-2007 helping residents of Gulfport, MS, recover from Hurricane Katrina. He enjoys volunteering with the Sierra Club to develop native plant landscape projects in public areas in Columbus, IN. Eric is very thankful to his sister, Suzanne, for moving to Boston and introducing Jen to him 14 years ago!*

Love Letter
Jen Riddle

Eric,

When we met, I had the advantage of knowing about your diagnosis and some of the challenges it caused you. Because your sister was my roommate, I had the privilege of praying you through some difficult times even before I met you. That gave me insight I never expected I was going to need in the future. When we started dating two years later, we never had to have the awkward conversation where you shared your diagnosis. When is a good time to do that, really?

But I walked into our relationship with a disadvantage that had nothing to do with you at all—my own hubris. I believed that your bipolar disorder would never be a challenge we couldn't overcome because I knew so much. As a psychology major in undergrad and grad school, as well as being a Board Certified Behavior Analyst, I knew a lot. Because of all that knowledge, I thought I knew how to deal with anything that bipolar could throw our way, and if I didn't know, I had the right resources to find out. I was wrong.

We had a lot of ups and downs in our dating life. You were my first serious relationship, and I had pretty big expectations. I knew I loved you early on, and I carried a lot of pent-up ideals about what one's path to the altar looked like. In the midst of all that, you were dealing with a number of emotional challenges from your first marriage, as well as trying to find your way in your occupational life.

We were engaged when you were in a depression, but it was such a thoughtful and memorable evening that really symbolized so much in our relationship. Our faith, the bittersweet nature of change and growth, as well as our love of connection over a great meal, were all celebrated that night. But you weren't 100% you. The depression held part of you locked inside. That was so hard to watch. There were many times that you expressed a lack of confidence in yourself, but I was so glad that I could see the real you—the compassionate, intelligent man who deeply cared for others. More than anything, this is what I wanted you to see in yourself, that you were valuable no matter what.

Less than six months after our wedding, your depression grew very deep. There were many times I was able to provide additional therapeutic help that got you through the day, but other days I was not. Things got worse when your sleep was consistently disrupted. I still thought I could help you manage what was happening, but felt increasingly unsure of our decisions regarding your mental health. It took some pivotal conversations with your parents, your mom in particular, to clarify that we needed to seek in-patient care.

That decision was a turning point in both our lives. Your short stay in the hospital helped you find a medication cocktail that supports you well and forced open doors for you to talk about your diagnosis. I learned that my knowledge has limits and helping to support your mental health takes a village. I could not support you alone.

We've walked through a lot in our nearly 11 years of marriage: the joy of road-trips, random dance parties that you reluctantly join, hundreds of hours of cheering for various sports teams, travel adventures that have taken us to fantastic locales, laughter about really silly things that can go on and on, and amazing concerts in unexpected places. This is not the end of our story. There are many more adventures to come, and I'm sure not all of them will seem lovely or good at the time. But one day, when we step back to look at our lives together, we will see that God has pieced together a beautiful mosaic from everything we thought were broken pieces.

Love Always,

Jen

Jen Riddle *is a family ministry pastor, currently serving at First Presbyterian Church in Columbus, Indiana. She is also a Board-Certified Behavior Analyst who has served children and families with autism for nearly 25 years. Jen loves to move her body with running and yoga and loves lifting heavy things! She is an avid reader who recently discovered the joy of crocheting amigurumi characters. Jen and Eric have been married for over 10 years, continuing to learn along the way what it means to care for one another through their sacred bond, providing flexibility for growth and support as each partner needs it.*

Dear Zach, From Coco

Courtney Diles

Dear Zach,

One day last summer, we were half-heartedly arguing about one of your doctor's appointments. I said that your needs mattered too, and you began to cry as if in relief.

That was when I knew I had messed up. I lost my ability to work; I lost friends; we lost our home; I lost my ability to trust my body, my brain, myself, and everyone else. I had been so lost in my sea of loss that I had let you think you mattered less.

We have spent so long pulling puzzle pieces together—suicidal thoughts, pure OCD, dissociative disorders, neurodivergences, diabetes, asthma, allergies, fibromyalgia, and more. Not everybody gets the privilege to spend a year healing like I just did. You made that happen for me.

And now that I am climbing back onto the shore, I want to sit here with you a minute like the night we met and write words in the sand.

Thank you.
I love you.
You matter.

And all of it more colossal and fathomless than the sea and sky colliding.

Coco

Courtney Diles *struggled with severe depression and anxiety for a decade. She had four hospitalizations and went through electroconvulsive therapy, but only seemed to get worse. She finally improved once she was* *treated for pure OCD and dissociative issues, which had become coping mechanisms in her struggle with chronic pain. With her mind finally peaceful, she is now on a journey to manage her fibromyalgia. Zach has stood with her through it all.*

Love Letter About My Brain Issue

Laura Moseley

My Dearest Shawn,

I wanted to write you a letter to let you know I love you more with each passing day and cannot believe that we've been together over three years now. I also want to thank you for being such a kind, laid-back, sweet, caring person—I honestly had no idea that men could be like that. During my previous (abusive) relationship, I was always led to believe that I was unlovable and not worthy of fulfilling companionship, which is clearly not true. I'm not sure what I did to deserve such love and devotion, but I am so beyond blessed that our paths crossed. It was truly the Hand of God!

I love how you wonder about and attend to mine and my kids' well-being. Perhaps it's me just gushing about what I love about you, but I love the fact that you value and respect my opinion, that you joke with me constantly and keep me laughing, that you push me to be the best version of myself, as well as call me out on my inconsistencies. You are understanding, but you are quick to tell me about the excuses I sometimes give. Again, I've never had anything remotely close to that kind of care from a significant other. You are not only my love but my best friend. Anytime anything happens, good or bad, I cannot wait to share it with you first!

I also know that the downsides of my TBI cause a shift in my cognitive function, so I am sometimes moody for no apparent reason. Some days, too, I cannot speak properly or order my thoughts. I know I forget the simplest things or repeat some things over and over. I didn't ask for a traumatic brain injury, but I have it and it often makes me feel like damaged goods—like you would do better to have a clear-headed significant other who could think on her feet. I assure you, even though I often feel too-much-trouble or "broken," I know I have to be kind to myself. I have to force myself to be gentle, especially when I remind myself that I could've died from the abuse I received. I'm sure being with me can sometimes not be easy or fun. Occasional irrational anxiety makes that condition worse, which I know you know all too well. I feel trapped in the jail cell of my brain issue. It's frustrating, but I try hard not to take that frustration out on you.

I used to be so organized, eloquent, and task-driven—I could get things handled like no one's business. I was structured and accomplished. Now all I feel like is messy and child-like, which can make me frustrated and emotional. I know you understand that completely, and I treasure that you're so laid back and sweet with me, taking everything in stride. I also adore the way you let me be my true self, even though I'm still rediscovering who that is at times. It is both startling and exciting how alike we are sometimes, in our morals and interests. It's uncanny, but also further illustrates how God knows best.

I just wanted you to know how special you are and to show my appreciation for the gentle tolerance you extend to me, always. I certainly wish our paths had crossed years ago. Think how more content and settled you and I would be by now! Here's to a continued long, long time together!

"There is no heart for me like yours." - Maya Angelou

All my love always,
Laura

Laura Moseley *is a single mother of three and grandmother of one, as well as a Domestic Violence/Sexual Violence survivor of over 23+ years of abuse. She works for a federal social services organization by day and as a certified DV advocate in the rest of her spare time. She is a writer, blogger, future podcaster, activist, and public speaker.*

To My Loving Husband from Your Grateful Wife

Moriah Couch

Dear Husband,

Living with depression and anxiety is like a constant battle with myself. The continuous flow of conflicting thoughts and emotions is exhausting. On the one hand, depression makes me lethargic and grumpy, depletes all motivation, and makes me not care about anything. On the other hand, anxiety makes me fidgety, unable to sit still, and all the emotions about everything flood in at once and it's too much to bear sometimes.

Feeling these two things simultaneously can be extremely confusing. There's a never-ending war taking place in my brain, and most days it takes everything I have just to manage that alone. That's not even taking into account the everyday tasks and responsibilities that all fall on my shoulders.

Being a wife, mother, raising three children with autism and ADHD, and managing my own mental health is quite a job. You know all of this. You know how I can't stand messes and clutter, yet how at the same time, the mess and clutter overwhelm me to the point that it causes panic attacks and I can't bring myself to clean. How between my own struggles and our children's struggles, there are times when I just need a break— to be alone and have time to regulate my own emotions.

With depression and anxiety come other symptoms like chronic pain and fatigue. My body feels foreign to me some days. The aches and pains and feeling physically sick can be all-consuming. Anxiety likes to amplify those symptoms, making me think I have some deadly disease, which sends me into panic attacks that leave me buried under the covers in bed, unable to function because of the irrational fears.

The constant feeling of exhaustion never really lessens or goes away. It doesn't matter how much or little sleep I get. It isn't that kind of tired. It's the kind of tiredness that goes so deep through your body and bones that no amount of rest can make up for it. I could sleep for 12 hours straight and still feel like I've been up for days. This is one of the many reasons why getting out of bed in the mornings is so difficult.

The funny thing is that depression and anxiety also cause insomnia. So even though I'm completely exhausted every day, I can never sleep at night. For whatever reason, nighttime is always the worst for my anxiety. I lie down to sleep and even though my body is ready to shut down, my brain never is. I can't turn it off. The thoughts come racing in, and there's no way to stop it.

All my worries and fears come crashing to the front and I lie there panicked, wishing desperately for sleep to come. It usually takes hours, and most nights I have to turn on a show to distract myself from my thoughts in order to sleep. When sleep finally comes, it is rarely peaceful. I toss and turn all night long. Nightmares regularly fill my dreams—the kind that feel so real that I awaken terrified and unable to fall back asleep. Basic tasks can seem daunting, so much so at times that I won't be able to do them at all.

Things like making a phone call, scheduling an appointment, going to the store, taking a shower, doing laundry or dishes—these things can seem impossible for me during the times when my mental health is in poor condition. Sometimes it's only a day or two, but other times it can last for months.

I can go weeks at a time without leaving the house or push off needed appointments for months. Sometimes I finally manage to schedule it but when the day comes, I can't bring myself to go, and I cancel at the last minute. Bathing feels like too much work when I'm struggling mentally, and it takes all my willpower to find the energy just to shower. Dishes and laundry often pile up due to having young children who make constant dirty dishes and laundry. I can't keep up and the overflowing sink and piles of clothes by the washer can be too overwhelming to manage.

Then add in raising our special needs children—dealing daily with meltdowns, stims, food aversions, aggression, manic behaviors—and I'm sure you can guess how that would have a negative impact on my already poor state of mental health. Don't get me wrong—I love our children more than anything and I'm so blessed to be their mom. But that doesn't mean it isn't hard. That doesn't mean it doesn't take everything I have to get through a day.

There was a time earlier in our relationship when you didn't understand these things. But over the years you have learned about depression and anxiety, and I'm so thankful for everything you do for me—how you love me through the storms and never give up on me. Not everyone is so lucky. You have done the work to learn about my struggles, to listen, to learn what I need during the hard times. You can now recognize the signs when I'm about to have a panic attack or when I'm falling into the dark abyss of depression.

You reassure and comfort me when the anxious thoughts have me spinning out of control. You Google things for me to find answers so that I don't have to because we both know Google is an anxious person's worst enemy. You help me with household chores and the kids when I'm overwhelmed and struggling so much as to get out of bed. You tell me to rest and take breaks, and you never resent me for my struggles. You pray for me and always remind me to look to God and everything He has brought us through when I feel like I'm drowning. I'm beyond grateful to have a partner in this life who truly loves and supports me, mental health illnesses and all.

Signed,
Your Wife

Moriah Couch writes, *"I am happily married to a hard-working and loving husband. A homeschooling SAHM to three beautiful children, one diagnosed with autism, and two diagnosed with both autism and ADHD. I'm a follower of Jesus on a journey of maintaining my own mental health through it all and sharing my experiences in the hopes of spreading awareness and encouraging others along the way. You can follow me on Facebook or Instagram @lifewiththecouches"*

To My Dearest Ann

Steve Fukunaga

To My Dearest Ann,

I am writing you this letter to express my thoughts about our relationship and how I feel about you personally.

For over 21 years, you have been my wife, best friend, and soul mate. I cannot imagine life without you. You are the reason I wake up each day thanking God I have you in my life. I live for you.

You went through a lot having to adjust to living in a very different culture. You left your home and family to start a life with me. I cannot tell you enough how much I appreciate the sacrifices you had to make to marry me and be my lifelong partner. I can never do enough to show you how much this means to me.

Over the past 21 years, we have learned a lot about each other. We are so different from each other, yet there is that attraction that draws us closer together. I guess the saying "opposites attract" is so true. In many ways our differences complement each other. Our weakness is supported by our strengths. We also have a lot in common, which allows us to do things together we both enjoy.

I've never understood the true meaning of having "unconditional love," but now I can truly say I know what it means when I say to you that my love for you is unconditional. I also know the feeling is mutual with you. For all the hard times I've given you and all the times I needed your help with my health issues, you stood by me and supported me without expectations. For this, I really appreciate you.

One of the things I've had to learn and adjust to is your depression and anxiety. This was a new thing I've never experienced before. It was difficult emotionally, but over time you have taught me how to cope with this condition. It is still not easy, but I now know what to do and what to say whenever you are having an episode. No matter what the situation is, I still love you and I will always stand by you and support you.

We've gone through a lot over the past 21 years, but we are still together putting up with our weirdness. If we can still laugh at each other, there will be joy!

The last thing I want to tell you is how you have helped me with my spiritual walk. You have influenced me with your dedication to reading the Bible and studying God's word. I had back-slidden so far away from following God, but over the years, I have come to realize that without God in our lives, we may not have made it this far. I thank God for His grace and blessings on our marriage. We have certainly lived the vows we took on June 11, 2000, "in sickness and in health, for richer and poorer."

I love you dearly,
Your "honey bunch of oats"
Steve

My Dearest Ladybug

Steven Lomelino

My Dearest Ladybug,

November 4, 2004, is a day we will never forget. To you, it was another normal weekday morning. To me, it was the last day of my life.

We had lived side by side for the two years prior to this, with you knowing I was still struggling to find employment that was as satisfying and financially rewarding as the one lost to the 1999 merger. What you didn't know was that I considered myself dead during that time. I didn't see it at the time, but my job, my self-worth, and my identity were so intertwined with my career that when it was lost, so was I.

I didn't know who I was anymore for all those years, yet I never told you. Instead, my misplaced resolve to recreate my past career success had me convinced that anything short of that was failure. It wasn't even a career failure in my mind. It was a complete life failure, and I was dragging you and our boys down with me into this unbearable existence.

You tried so hard to get me to see the good that remained for us to enjoy after the merger. Despite your best efforts, all I could see was the struggle the financial loss was causing. That was combined with a work environment that compounded my thoughts of being a failure, which was pulling me down from depression into despair. Again, I couldn't vocalize to you that having no good options was tormenting my mind. Staying in a bad work environment and losing my sanity, or leaving and losing everything, were circling endlessly through my mind with you right next to me. I chose to find a way to avoid both without even letting you know how much each day of work was eroding what little hope I had left.

Then, on November 3rd, I made my plans to escape. Death was my main thought, with disappearing as a secondary thought. Again, we were side by side, and I said nothing. A feigned normal goodbye the next morning could have been our last, and I said nothing because I was set on following through with my plans. That is exactly what I did until God intervened.

After a round trip to "remote," I faced the big question. Did I want to talk to you? After not including you in a way that could have prevented me from trying to end my life, for years, did I now want to talk to you? At that very moment, my answer was no. Deep inside, I did want to talk to you. But in the condition I was in after my suicide attempt, knowing I had made a huge mistake leaving you out, I simply couldn't.

Eventually, we were face to face. I expected anger, condemnation, and a lot of questions that I had no answers to. I also expected to hear, "I didn't sign up for this" from you. I got much of what I expected. Yet, despite me blindsiding you with nearly ending my life, you still loved me. I felt totally unworthy of anyone loving me after all the years of hiding what was really going on with me behind lies and going through the motions. Your love was the last thing I expected to not have to earn back.

When you visited me in the hospital, I tried to convince you that staying with me was a bad idea. You stayed anyway. Many women would have taken that easy out and bailed. Your perfect balance of compassion and understanding with expectations and truth breathed life back into me.

Now, here we are in 2023, celebrating 37 years of marriage. It has been anything but what either of us thought we signed up for. I was never able to re-create my past career success. We've had two actual vacations because our vacation money is paying for the surgeon's and many other medical professionals' vacations, and it's hard to navigate the challenges life keeps presenting us with.

We've gone through it all together since that nearly tragic November 4th day, though. No more stuffing my emotions inside because I feel I'm failing you. No more excluding you from hard situations and decisions—all because I know there is nothing that will change how much you love me.

Always and forever the love of your life!
Steven

Steven Lomelino *is first and foremost a Christian. His relationship with Christ became much deeper after living through loss, injustice, depression, and suicidal despair. Through this, he found Christ was the only source of lasting hope. Then the call to share this journey with others came. Initially, this was as a group leader to give back to the mental health group that had helped him recover. God kept calling him to share with more people by putting his story on paper. He composed the book* Insane Success.

My Heart's Hero

Tina Guthmiller

Tim,

"There's something I should tell you. I'm bipolar."

You said, "Okay." You weren't scared. You didn't question it.

I said, "I'm hard to love."

You said, "No, you aren't."

I said, "I hate myself more than I hate people."

You said, "That's okay. I hate people too, and I love you enough for both of us."

I said, "I have chronic suicidal thoughts."

You asked, "Why?"

I said, "Because of my illness—it's part of my illness! So I'm pretty sure that's how I'm going to die. Just don't blame yourself. It's nobody's fault. It's the illness. I'm sick."

You asked, "What can I do to help?"

I said, "Don't egg me on when I'm pissed. Don't scream back. Don't give me a reason to freak out."

You asked again, "What can I DO to help?"

I said, "There is one rule for you and the kids . . . You can ask me if I've taken my meds and I CAN'T get mad."

(You've asked me, you have brought them to me, and you have driven me to the pharmacy if I'm out.)

"One other thing you can do and the kids can do is tell me to take a nap. Sometimes I just need a nap. I'm like a toddler that way."

You said, "Okay."

I said, "I can't handle a checkbook. I can't handle money."

You said, "Okay."

You handle the money, but we are married and my name is on the accounts. My brain can't decipher real cash from digital banking. It's fine for a while and then I impulsively take money that should be for bills. My mind can't make that connection. I constantly scramble trying to make up for my mistakes. I say I always have a plan. Trust me. You have learned those are famous words of my illness talking. "I'm so sorry" is all I ever say. I think I expect you to leave me after every episode and yet you don't. I tell you to leave, as I will destroy you. You said, "Money doesn't matter. We can live on less. We will be okay."

I don't like to cook much. I don't like to clean. I get distracted when I try to do any projects. You have noticed this. You compliment me when I get a load of laundry done, make a meal, or clean the kitchen. You compliment me because even though you don't live inside my brain, you see the limitations it puts on me.

I have brought in two more dogs since we've been together. You grudgingly allowed them, but your heart is full of love for them now. You have witnessed how therapeutic they are for both of us. I love you for that. They love you.

I advocate for people with disabilities and I have strong principles in other things. You never question my motives, and you are first and foremost to protect me when others have hurt me. If I'm unreasonable you explain to me why I am. You don't get angry.

You come with me to watch the grandkids or help when they are at our house. One night one of them got the stomach flu and I had to clean them up and cuddle, clean up and cuddle. We got in the truck to go home and you said, "Good job, grandma."

I said, "Huh?"

You said, "You handled that like a trouper!"

I said, "Thanks."

I thought about it and realized you never saw me when my kids were real little. It was special that you noticed.

I have asked you many times why you stay. You said because you love me. We laugh every day. You said, "What would I do without you?"

Every heart has a hero. You are my heart's hero, Tim. I love you.

Tina Guthmiller writes, *"Mental illness is generational in my family, so I am an advocate as well as a person with an SMI.*

Chapter 4. To the Siblings

To My Little Brother, Mark

Catherine J. Rippee-Hanson

Dear Mark,

I have learned so much from you. Despite experiencing tremendous pain, it is still possible to find incredible joy. No, I am not saying your serious mental illness is a blessing. As a testament to your experience, that would be almost sacrilegious. However, certain realizations that I have come to because of your life circumstances have changed me for the better. I am less judgmental. I'm brave. Having learned certain characteristics from someone who has endured great struggle, I am able to step out of my comfort zone with confidence. I am aware of the importance of community. It is essential that everyone has a tribe to keep them going and to encourage them. And you do have support from our community. It is possible for me to be a warrior despite my own limitations. Due to my love for you, I can stand up and advocate for you with confidence and boldness.

We are dealing with mental illness as a family, even though it stole away all sense of normalcy for our family and has turned our lives upside down. There was no way we could have known what had hit us. Fear or lack of knowledge caused many friends to walk away. Throughout your long struggle, you have been abandoned by many family members who do not understand how severe or uncontrollable your illness and symptoms are. I cannot turn away from you. A sister does not let her brother suffer, does not sit back and watch her brother in pain without doing something . . . anything . . . to make it better. I am still here to protect you, even if you cannot see me, despite the social constraints that prevent me from doing more.

Many of us, including myself, can embrace two complete opposites at the same time. There are moments of joy and moments of pain. Even though there are tears, there is still laughter. My current strength comes from the memories from the past and the hope for the future, even when there is distance. It is possible to remain grateful despite difficult circumstances. If you reach out and hold my hand, however rarely, I am reminded that you are still around and that you still love me, even if you are suffering from mental illness. I have gratitude for those moments when I glimpse you through the veil of your illness.

Sometimes it can be confusing, frightening, and exhausting. Often it seems that the anger you feel toward the world is personal, but I know it is just the nature of the illness. In a world where we often take what we have for granted, it is sometimes difficult to see or understand what you are going through or experiencing. Observing your distress can be difficult at times, and I am often consumed by agony myself. Constant worry, unpredictability, and the knowledge that I have no control to make it better for you break me in unimaginable ways, draining the very essence of my energy.

I understand that you are unable to comprehend the impact of your behavior due to the symptoms of your illness. Although you are ill, your value in my life is not diminished, but rather it makes me treasure the memories of who you once were. All the memories we shared are still fresh in my mind, and it hurts me to think you are so alone.

In our childhood you would sneak around and give me a fright, playing practical jokes all the time. There is an unbreakable bond between us. Don't think that I don't care about you, brother. Neither the past nor the future will change. I am pained to see what you must deal with. It hurts even more because there's nothing I can do. I just wish I could make it all okay, but all I can do is pray. You used to smile at me when you looked at me for answers to your unending questions. I can still see you grinning from ear to ear. And now all I can say is, "Life isn't always fair."

I remember the little boy who, at three years old, insisted on going to the store with me and clung to my hand. I remember the young boy, at the age of seven, with whom I fished in the river and caught tadpoles in creek beds while you exclaimed in the moment, proudly, "That is my sister!" I will never forget, after moving out on my own, the 12-year-old boy who tracked me down at a neighbor's house where I was visiting a friend, and tearfully, unabashedly pleaded with me to move back home. You couldn't understand why I moved away. The upbeat teenager who was always bragging about how many girlfriends you had and how someday you would marry and have a family of your own. A young man who sought my advice and turned to me for guidance when he was confused about his life. Your belief in me never wavered. I wish I had all the answers you were looking for.

While most would consider your situation insurmountable, I acknowledge in amazement your strength and resilience. Understanding hopelessness is an experience I empathize with, as is knowing that the mentally ill experience it daily. With all that psychosis and mental illness can bring to your life, it's a testament to your courage that you manage to get through each day and night.

It is most important to me that you know I love you. I will always love you. It doesn't matter how trapped you are in psychosis and delusions of fear and anger—I love you. As the world turns its back on you and shuts its eyes, I still see you. I know in my heart who you are. Who you always have been. Who you will always be. My little brother.

Your loving sister,
Catherine J. Rippee-Hanson

Catherine J. Rippee-Hanson writes, *"My background is that of a lifelong social activist, serious mental illness advocate, and writer— navigating tragedies while advocating for and challenging our broken mental healthcare system. Through my advocacy and lived experience witnessing the barriers we encountered for my brother before his death, I have developed a deep understanding of the systemic inequalities that exist within our mental healthcare system, which motivated me to bring attention to these issues and to fight for reform."*

A Promise I Can Keep

Linda (Rippee) Privatte

To my younger and only brother, Mark,

I grew up believing that love could fix anything . . . that love conquers all. That love would carry us through any situation. I believed that family never gives up on family. I had always been accused of being too emotional for my own good. I was devastated and in shock over your original motorcycle accident that happened in 1987, when you lost a third of your frontal lobe in a massive Traumatic Brain Injury. Your head, face, and jaw were wired back together. Metal plates were put in your head. A metal rod was placed in one leg and what we thought was the worst of it was you lost both of your eyes. The doctors told us you would have brain damage from the TBI and if you lived, you would be 100% blind permanently.

I stood outside the doors of the ER with Dad after many doctors told him they weren't sure they could save you. He expressed to me from a very dark place that he wasn't sure that they should save you. We all thought blindness was going to be the big tragedy in your life. Dad worried that you were not strong enough to adapt to your life sightless. Your ability to deal with blindness was almost your superhuman power. You amazed us. We were told you would have brain damage, but we didn't comprehend what that would mean for you. We could not have foreseen that your future would come to include a serious brain disorder just a few years later. The anosognosia has been a hurdle we haven't been able to get over. We were so naïve. I so wish we knew then what we know now!

That night outside the ER, I begged Dad not to give up on you. I expressed my love for you, my only brother. I thought we could love you through anything. Dad told me that all I would ever have to offer you is love, and that love would never be enough. I didn't want his words to be true. I still don't. Love might not save you, but I will always offer it to you. Promises were made to you and all with good intentions. No one in the family knew then about serious mental illness or the wreck of a mental health system we would face in attempting to navigate and to advocate for you and your care over three decades. We could not have imagined that the last 14 years you would be homeless with anosognosia and no treatment for your no-fault brain disease. I would have never believed that our laws would prevent our family from seeking treatment that you so desperately needed. For over 20 years we managed to care for you, but when you became homeless and the anosognosia prevented you from accepting help is when I really began to understand the depths of the battle you were facing.

I'm so sorry for the broken promises that became impossible to keep. Always and forever lasts a long time. Now my promises sound empty to you. These broken promises keep me awake at night as you sleep on the streets, blind, with serious mental illness, and as broken as my promises. I have so many apologies to make to you. I'm sorry that we made impossible promises to you that we would never be able to keep and that others prevented us from keeping.

I'm sorry that a true and accountable mental health system does not exist for those with SMI. I regret that I have not been able to remove any of those barriers that have prevented your care. I'm sorry for the fear and danger you live in daily and especially your pain and suffering. You deserve to receive treatment like any other person with a physical disease. I'm so sorry for the SMI that is the overwhelming darkness in your life, more so than the blindness. I feel the need to apologize to you for the world we live in that would allow your situation to continue without acknowledging that changes are necessary. I love you. I'm trying to keep you safe and I apologize for the inadequate job I have done. So many people have harmed you.

I have found you on the streets and been your Curbside Caregiver for 14 years now. When you were a child, you would always look at me with your silly, boyish grin and say, "Please, please, Linda, if you love me!" It always seemed to work for any request. I couldn't say, "No." Your needs out on the streets have you using that same plea to me, "Please, please, Linda, if you love me!" No silly grin now, just desperation in your pleading. I do love you and that's why I keep searching to find you, to care for you, and fight the injustice of mental health laws at the same time. I'm trying to keep you alive with my care. Please forgive us for the mental health system that continuously collapses on our backs, ties our hands, and blindfolds us through HIPAA. I'm so sorry for the discrimination, the inadequacies, the ignorance, and the lack of empathy that you face on a daily basis.

Dad might have been right that my love would not be enough, but I still keep coming to you and offering my love. I keep finding you. I keep fighting for you. I keep seeking the treatment you need. I keep loving you and making sure you know it. Maybe love is the only thing that lasts always and forever . . . not promises. At the public meeting where I spoke publicly for the first time, I told Solano County that I would make sure they knew your name, they would come to know your story, and I would be back to tell them the end of your story. . . a promise that I will keep.

I love you. A promise I can keep.
Your sister, Linda

Linda (Rippee) Privatte writes, *"The tragic life of my brother, leading up to his death with untreated mental illness, inspired me to become an advocate for people suffering from serious mental illness or brain disorders (SMI/SBD). In my case, I was one of the many 'Curbside Caregivers' who go out into the streets to care for loved ones who are unable to care for themselves and are struggling with similar issues that my brother faced and advocating for their right to treatment."*

Dear Ann Marie

Mary Beth Honsinger

Dear Ann Marie,

As I think of the holiday season, the end of the year, and the beginning of the new year, I know how blessed I am having you by my side. I could not ask for a better sister.

You always seem to know when I'm getting close to leaping in the rabbit hole of depression and anxiety, and you catch me by the tail. It may be a cup of coffee, a delicious homemade meal, or a walk together to just bring us together to talk and see where I am on my journey. You always look to see how you might help me get out of my own way.

I don't know where I would be without your love, gentle nudge, and artful sight. Thank you for being you and for loving me when I feel unlovable.

I love you,
Mary Beth

Dear Carla

Trez Buckland

Dear Carla,

As my eldest sister, you had a special part in raising me. Thank you for all you did to encourage me, especially through my teen years and early college. You were so thoughtful with my friends—willing to give us rides when we needed them in high school. I will never forget the day we got into the car accident when the young lady ran the stop sign—we flipped three times! It was amazing we only had cuts and bruises and were able to walk home from the site. I thank you and the '57 Chevy for that. You kept your cool and kept us calm.

And then moving on to my college years—did you realize how much it meant that you would drop me off at the university on your way to work every day? You must have had much on your mind as you were heading off to be with your kindergarten class, but you kindly took time to listen to me all the way until you dropped me off.

Eventually I graduated, married, and had little ones of my own. All through the years, after you moved farther away, you never ceased to send us cards and letters. That was you—always thinking of the other person. After you passed on, I gladly accepted all your unused stationery and cards and try to keep up your tradition of writing to others. You were certainly the patron saint of letter writing.

You also were the queen of the telephone. I can only imagine your long-distance calling bill! I remember our last conversation so well—you were in the hospital with pneumonia. You were going to be going home the next day. I was so happy for you. Because I didn't want to have you run up your bill I said, "I'd better let you go now." You responded urgently— "No—don't let me go!" We talked a little more, saying our sweet good-byes, only to find out the very next day that you never made it out of the hospital—you were taken home to Heaven as you slept. Your legacy is love.

Love,
Your sister, Trez

Dear Paula

Trez Buckland

Dear Paula,

It has been 20 years now since you left this world. We all miss you terribly. The day you left is permanently etched into my memory, but along with that sorrow comes the joy of remembering you. How I wish I had told you more what a gift you were to us all.

You were the favorite "Auntie" to the boys. Who else would put up with their shenanigans as you did? Who else would invite them overnight? Who else would have them come for swimming parties? Who else would take the time to potty train them with special stuffed animals? They gloried in your attention. They laughed and smiled every time you came over. You had nothing but happiness to give them and you gave it without holding back.

Your energy and enthusiasm were so special. You were the best babysitter ever. We have your picture forever and always with our family photo collage up on the wall. This way our newest family additions—all the grandchildren—can know your smile, too, and hear tell of the favorite "Auntie." I only wish you could have all met.

Your life was always full of excitement and adventure as you reached out in friendship to so many people over the years—artists, poets, musicians, cooks, everyday folks from young to old.

Our last weekend together was bittersweet—celebrating a 21st birthday for my youngest son, your youngest nephew, celebrating Father's Day, and spending time at our favorite place in the world—the cabin. We did yard work together, cooked together, ate together, and played games until 1:00 in the morning. The last one was Scrabble. You gave and gave of yourself to us all. I wish I could rewind that weekend and push pause so that we could play again and continue our lives together. Know that we will never forget you. Your legacy is love.

Love,
Your sister, Trez

Dear April

Tony Roberts

Dear April,

I want to tell a story I've told many times before. But I can't tell it enough. It's the story of what happens when someone with a mental illness falls into the pit of despair and is lifted up by the loving faithfulness of one who cares.

December 1, 2016. I am in the Goodman exit lane off I-490 in Rochester, New York. An unusual light shines in my rearview. In seconds, I hear a loud crack and feel a tremendous lurch. Someone traveling too close, going too fast, hit me. Hard.

I called 911 and a policeman showed up, followed by an ambulance. I was taken to Strong Memorial Hospital where they ran tests and found nothing conclusive. But I became increasingly agitated. I became convinced that I was paralyzed. Three doctors ran tests on me at separate times and concluded that nothing was wrong. Physically.

That's when I called you.

You lived in Indiana, 500 miles away from that Emergency Department at Strong in Rochester, New York. It was almost midnight. But you calmly listened to me. Even when I told you I was receiving no care. Even when I told you I was contacting my lawyer to sue the hospital.

You listened. You didn't try to convince me my confused thoughts were illogical. Instead, you advocated for me, calling the ED nurses' station to explain to them that I was having a manic episode, that I was not on drugs, that I wasn't like this, that I needed psychotropic meds and psychiatric care.

In time, I was transferred to a psychiatric unit. I was given medication. But it took a while to take effect. My emotions were raw. I cried. Then laughed. Yelled. Then apologized. Cried some more. They asked me if I wanted to call anyone.

I called you.

You asked how I was doing. I bawled. Before I could get a word out, you said, "I will come, if you want me to." I didn't want to ask you. You have a family. A job. A home.

Again, you asked, "Do you want me to come?"

I was so overwhelmed. Now, all the emotions I had felt were absorbed into one. Gratitude.

It was nearly 6 a.m. when I got off the phone. By 6 p.m., you walked into my room carrying a Starbucks coffee and a bag of chocolate espresso beans.

Loving faithfulness. It's hard to find in a world filled with unconcern. But each time it happens, it is a miracle. God working through angels to pull us out of pits, to show us hope, to shine light in the darkness.

Chapter 5. To God, Self, and Others

Creative Genius in the Midst of Mental Illness
Alison Lammot

Growing up with a mother who hid under the covers battling her bipolar disorder made me grow up fast. As the oldest, I had to help take care of the four other kids. When she gave up her battle at age 38, I was a senior in high school and dropped out to take care of the kids.

Where did my childhood go? I was angry at her . . . until I got into my twenties and the depression started to hit me also. It is like going into a dark tunnel, and you do not know if you will make it to the other end. Luckily, during that time, I found light in my encounter with God.

But dealing with humans was much harder. No one can understand the amount of energy, patience, and courage it takes to get through one day with mental illness. I also had a bad car accident at age 23 and had a TBI on top of PTSD and depression. My mother never had the option for help from medication and was shamed for her mental illness.

By the time mine showed up, there were lots of meds and a better understanding and acceptance of the struggles we go through. Doctors are learning new things about the brain every day. I look forward to seeing the amazing breakthroughs that are coming and will hopefully set us free from darkness and pain. In the meantime, the dark times in the cave are when I write my best poems and songs! Creative genius often lives in the middle of a mental illness. . .

Alison Lammot *is an Educator, Counselor, Life Coach, Author and Speaker.*

Dear Fellow Traveler

Brandon Appelhans

Dear Fellow Traveler,

Did you think life was going to go like this? You had plans and dreams about work, life, accomplishments, where you wanted to live and with whom. Then mental illness stepped in. Now what?

I was 14 when the darkness fell on me. I was a freshman: insecure, loud, loving, caring, smart, prideful, naïve, hopeful, occasionally hardworking, unfocused, etc. I played drums in bands, played goalie in soccer, and played Risk with my friends, sometimes for days.

Then I was nothing. I was a contaminant. I was walking in anguish.

I got home every day and carried myself upstairs to my room. I would turn on the radio, collapse into my comforter, and sob. The music drowned out the crying so no one else could hear.

I was not alone. Kay Redfield Jameson had bipolar disorder, like I do, and she survived. She had become a clinical psychologist and written books about her experience. I read her books and was taken with one thought: If she could survive, maybe I could too. So, I went to work staying alive. I was a good client for my mental health professionals. I took my meds. The rest was a blur.

It took two years to find effective meds. Then the world opened back up. I began to see the vibrancy of life around me again. I began to feel happiness. I felt alive.

After years of therapy and work with people with mental illness, I wish I could go back to 14-year-old me and share a few things.

You are still you inside.

I felt like I was living on the other side of a plate glass window, separate and isolated from the world. I was unable to interact. I felt intense pain, and my pain could consume me as the world continued to exist on the other side of the glass.

You are still you inside. Bipolar disorder took so much from me during those years, but inside I was still Brandon. It took every bit of my strength, creativity, spark, and perseverance to stay alive. My traits and skills were repurposed for survival.

During those two years, my life was on hold. My life resumed when I found the right meds and I worked to catch up on what I had missed. Mental illness cost me my sophomore and junior years of high school, but I got back the rest of my life.

Whatever your mental illness may cost you, you are still you.

Do your best. Release the rest.

Your best is probably worse than some of your worst days before. Mine was. Give 100% of what you have. That is enough for today. You may not have all the capacity you have enjoyed, but you will again.

Release the expectation that you need to be as productive as you were before mental illness. You may miss the honor roll, the promotion, the quota. You might miss them all. I did. I did not design my life before mental illness with enough space to go through suicidal ideation for two years. It is okay that you cannot meet every expectation you did before mental illness affected you. Give yourself some grace.

Take your meds. Be honest with your team.

You have a great shot at getting your life back. To do that, take your meds and give your team a chance. Your psychiatrist is making educated guesses about your brain chemistry. If you do not take your meds as prescribed and communicate, they cannot help you. Your psychologist or therapist is trying to heal your mind. They cannot help you unless you are honest with them, and you engage in the process.

Be honest. Take your pills. Follow your professionals' advice. Communicate.

Whatever that takes, do it. This is your lifeline. Take it seriously. When things do not work, communicate and keep trying.

You are good.

When I started showing the symptoms of bipolar disorder, I thought I was going to see a psychiatrist, get pills, and be better, instantly! We started medications. The days turned into weeks, months, and years. That grind eroded any sense of hope I had. I learned I did not just hate the disorder, I hated myself.

After years of therapy, I began to understand that I matter just because I exist. The creator of the universe really does think you are the best thing ever. It is part of being human, and nothing can take that away. When God thinks of you, He smiles, laughs, and loves.

You were good. You are good. You will be good. I know you may not believe it now, but it is true.

You can make it.

My psychiatrist thought I was going to die by suicide in 1999. I am still here. Did it suck? Yes, but I made it.

I still have bipolar disorder. I still take my pills, meet with my therapist, exercise regularly, and eat well to manage it. Now, 22 years later, I have a wife, two kids, a house, and we've started or owned three businesses in the last ten years. I was never supposed to enjoy all of this, but I do.

If I can make it, you can too. You are stronger and better than you know. Just keep going. It is worth every bit. I promise.

Dear Friend or Family Member

Brandon Appelhans

Editor's Note: warning—graphic details of a suicide attempt.

If you or someone you know is thinking about suicide, please call 988 for the 988 Suicide and Crisis Lifeline or text the word HOME or START to 741741 for the Crisis Text Line.

I bet it has been hard recently. Every day might feel like you are going to set them off. What would they do? I had guesses. I hoped my guesses were wrong: self-harm or a suicide attempt. I just wanted to keep her alive until something, anything, could change for the better. Maybe that would mean she could get back to who she was before.

I know what it is to come home and think your loved one is gone. That they finally did what they had mentioned, half kidding but completely serious. The car was gone out of the driveway when I got dropped off. She'd talked about how she would do it. Had she? Instantly, searing pain pulsed through me. Fear, agony, and loss welled up inside. I couldn't process it. I started to go numb. It was too much. How could she be gone? And then I heard the lock on the door click. She set her keys on the table and walked leisurely into the house, completely oblivious to the panic I had been in only minutes earlier. She looked into my eyes and saw the panic, relief, and fear. She asked, "Are you okay?"

I wanted to see her like I had before her depression. She would smile, laugh, and play. There was hope, beauty, and love in the world. Those were not just memories, right? I wanted those times again. I did not know if they would return, or if this reality, darkened by depression, was all there was left.

I would spring up in the middle of the night because I heard a noise. Was she trying to die? I was always on edge because I knew how serious it was. I felt so alone.

You are not alone. Your pain looks different than mine, but we know how much this journey hurts. We keep doing it because we hope they will be themselves again.

Every day you show up, research new ways to heal, look for resources, take initiative, build bridges, navigate systems, find support networks, and when you cannot find a way, you make one. You are a superhero without a cape and your superpower is hope. You are a lifeline. You are incredible. In your pain you keep going because they are worth it.

Sometimes it might feel like your world is unraveling, and your presence is the only thing keeping the darkness away. You are falling apart and keeping everything together simultaneously. I did. I did not have to show up perfectly all the time. I just had to show up. I could do my best to try to stay healthy enough to continue fighting, because this is a long fight.

Having been through this fight, please, do not try to support your loved one alone. Take care of yourself. Find your people. Take walks or runs. Work the stress out of your body. Pray and be seen. Hope when it feels silly and laugh when it is hard. Cry when the tears come. Let yourself grieve the life you used to have, and hope for a tomorrow that feels brighter than today. Give yourself permission to need and get therapy and help. Do all these things with people who love you. Do them for yourself and for the people you love. This battle is too long and hard otherwise.

I do not need to tell you to keep going, lasting, hoping, and trying. You will because you love them. I do need to tell you to take care of yourself. This is not a sprint or even a marathon. It is a marathon every day until you stop running. You are playing for time right now. If you give your loved one, the docs, the therapists, and the process time, it can work. You just need to last.

I was somebody's marathons. I'm still alive because of them. They loved recklessly and hoped boldly, even when it seemed futile. I am still here 23 years after my psychiatrist told my parents that I probably would not last until Christmas. Someone ran for me, and I give them credit for me still being here.

Then I got to run marathons for someone. I slogged through on scraps of grit and hope. She is still here, in part because I did not give up, and in part because my team ran with me: Mark, Anthony, Clint, Michael, John, and Stephen.

I signed up to run marathons for a friend. He died by suicide. I did all I could, but he did not want my help. I miss him.

Keep loving recklessly and hoping boldly. You cannot control the outcome, but your effort is critical. The world still has joy in it. You will see and participate in it again. Keep going and taking care of yourself.

Thank you for running the marathons for someone. You are not alone. You are incredible. Find your team and keep running together. As someone who had marathons run for me, and who is a fellow marathoner in this mental health fight, thank you.

Brandon

For All Who Have Cared for Me

Bob Holmes

To those who have cared for me:

To the caring staff of the hospital that took a young 18-year-old under their care after he tried to end his life. To the nurses and doctors who helped me find a reason for my mixed-up feelings and convinced me to keep fighting. They didn't know what I knew years later that gave me hope to carry on. I didn't then, but if I could go back, I would have told them thank you from the bottom of my heart for helping me.

To my parents, who must have worried many years through sleepless nights about my moodiness and thoughtless attitude toward people and things. How could anyone put up with someone who is so self-centered? I didn't want to go to school or anywhere, but they pushed me in a positive direction and kept after me to finish high school and a year of college. I thank them and only after I had my own kids did I learn of the sacrifices they made for me.

I married my high school sweetheart, and her mother was a high school counselor. She could see that I was still struggling with mental health issues and encouraged me to go to counseling. I was going downhill with work and family stresses and struggling with depression. I owe my life to my wife and her mother. I saw a counselor for several years and finally, after several medication trials and guidance, I asked what or why I was going through this. The counselor told me he thought that I was manic-depressive. He gave me hope by helping me with medication and with how to find ways to manage my life so I could lead a more normal life. I owe a large debt to my wife, her mother, and the therapist who stuck by me.

I was married for 21 years and we had many good years and three kids, but I had a hard time sticking to my meds, a steady sleep pattern, and exercise. I fell out of step with my wife. She had had enough and we divorced. Looking back many years later, she was a saint to put up with me for so long. I'm grateful to her and all those family and friends who helped me make it 45 years and taught me to be a better human and able to make better financial decisions so I could make it through one more divorce and on my own for another 26 years.

You Are a Superhero!
Cat Wolting

Hello, friend! I want to share a fact about me that is always on my mind. You see, I have a superpower. It took me 20 years to come to this realization. I have Bipolar II, anxiety, and ADHD. Notice I didn't say "I am." I refuse to let those terms define me as a superhero. But I digress.

These illnesses alter the way you think and process information. We think in a unique way which, once I realized this, caused me to appreciate these diagnoses where I hadn't ever before. Sometimes it's not very helpful, but more often than not, I am able to use these powers for good.

Because of my superpower, I am able to come up with solutions to problems that those without this power will rarely come up with. Now that I have embraced this and the superhero in me, I am successful at work, at home, and in life. There is no stopping me now!

It is my most sincere hope that you learn to embrace the superpowers you have to make your diagnosis work for you, instead of the constant battle between you and them. Never forget you are a superhero!

Cat Wolting writes, *"It took 21 years of significant suffering to receive the correct diagnosis. I advocate with the hope that, one day, no one else will be forced to suffer the way I did."*

Dear Suitor

I may be your second love in this lifetime, but know that in my heart, I always cherish the love you have for your one and first true love.

You narrated me your life despite the mental challenges you faced. You pushed me away to protect me from you falling again in the mental health ward. I do not even have any news of how you are today. I am hopeless since I lost your whereabouts, but I know that you talk to my picture every day. . . in your moments of darkness trying to replicate the advice, warmth, and comfort that I would enshrine you with when I was by your side.

However, you just keep living in my heart and know that I pray for your welfare wherever you are.

None of this can change my mind of your goodness despite how your surroundings perceive you. The loss of your first love was the grief that burst open your hallucinations and depressive behavior. The gates and doors you opened to cope were only acts of love.

I am sure that he is your guardian angel now above. One of my God's wishes is that both of you are reunited one day and complete your love story.

You once said to me the world is now a hell, and I am the only one who makes it worth it. I do not know if you hallucinate me alone or together with your first love, but know that we pray for your recovery even if we are miles away from you . . .

In your own ways, you said we are the complete opposite of each other despite not having met each other, and that you keep looking for others with our traits. It is only love that will uplift you forward despite what the other lovers can share with you.

You loved too much purely, but nothing can change how much I appreciate you.

There are moments when I miss you and moments when I fear the worst about you. I prepare myself daily, but nothing is short compared with what I feel.

As your only light on earth, I will always have my heart to hand out to you.

Please remember that I accompany you in your everyday battlefield,

From the other Al

Worthy of Love
Amanda Woodward

Dear Self,

You are doing an amazing job of looking normal. You have looked normal for years. Only those closest to you know that something is not right, but even they don't know the depths of your despair. It's time to make big changes.

Since your suicide attempt two years ago and your Covid illness, you have only existed on autopilot. You are paying the bills, but you are dead inside. You realize, don't you, that every day you go to work there are triggers that remind you of your failed attempt at death, and the hospitalization where you received very poor care.

You have asked your patients if they feel suicidal and at that very moment wished to die yourself. You have administered compassion along with every pill. In the worst, most critical times in those lives, you have been a little spark. Yes, you.

In the emergency department, the prison system, and the psychiatric hospitals, you calmly and kindly attend to people who need help. You have made a difference. A psychiatric nurse is who you are. But you are also a patient. You also need compassion.

It is time to reclaim your life. It's time to do those things you have advised others to do for 25 years. You must stop looking for others to show kindness to you for your own self-worth. You are worthy of love, Amanda, like the meaning of your name implies. You are lovely.

You must seek help and healing from childhood traumas that have left you fiercely independent. You must mother yourself like you have mothered four boys who love you very much. Your mother can never help with that. You know she had problems too. It wasn't your fault. You know that your father had problems and died too early because of them. That wasn't your fault either. You must not handle your problems as he did. You see where that led.

Self, if there's any wisdom in anything I have just said, please, please get the help you have needed for so long. You are going to have grandchildren one day, and your mission on this earth will continue—but only if you are truthful and honest with yourself. Be kind and compassionate to yourself.

And for a little pick-me-up, listen to that song by Miley Cyrus, "Flowers." There is a reason you love that song.

With all my love,
Amanda

Amanda Woodward *is a psychiatric nurse with 25 years of work in the emergency department, criminal justice system, and acute psychiatry. Her battle with major depression has been lifelong. She has managed it with medications and has been functional most of that time.*

Unending Grace

Grace Goodman

Where to begin? I was young and fragile, yet I felt like I could conquer the world! I was naïve and immature. Who could have blamed me? I was only 12 years old. One day my life changed forever—yes, even at that young age. And after that day, Nothing Was the Same. In fact, everything was very different and not in the way that it should be.

I'm not exactly sure what happened, but I can tell you the trigger that started it all. I was in fourth grade. I was sitting in class, and my teacher said something along the lines that if we didn't do our best or weren't perfect, God would smite us down! I don't really know whether she said this or if the devil just made me confused but, either way, that day fear—death-gripping fear—entered my life. I went to the bathroom and started having all these weird obsessions about how to use the restroom and how to wash my hands and how to drink and how to eat. I started worrying about things that no 12-year-old should have to worry about.

The stress of such obsessing began to build over time without anyone knowing what torment I was in. Yes, it was pure torture! Why do we put ourselves through unnecessary conditions just because we feel a certain way? Our feelings are fickle. I found that out along life's way. Yet my feelings and my emotions were full of fear and anxiety which eventually led to a deep depression.

As time went on, my brain began to experience more intense problems—problems that eventually led to utter chaos. When I was in 8th grade, I had a psychotic episode. Unfortunately, this was only the beginning of a much more traumatic road that was to come. What do you do when your whole world flips upside down and leaves you hanging in the wind? How do you respond when your mind is circling the drain? How do you live when your emotions and feelings are so overwhelmingly painful all you can hope for is a better day or that you'll just die so you don't have to experience it anymore?

It's not a way out that I wanted; it was a way to end the pain that so drastically devastated my mind, body, and soul. Why would such an optimistic and joyful girl who loved Jesus and accepted him at age four turn into such a mess? Why would she go from an athletic soccer player to a 300-lb vegetable? How could she turn into a pure anxiety-driven, psychosis-ridden human that never existed before? How could she go through so much pain that all she could think about was hope that Jesus would bring her to heaven to end all the grief and all the torture of the emotional and physical pain she was enduring?

Well, I'll tell you one way. She knew she had a purpose in this world and she knew God had a reason for what she was going through. Her faith in God kept her breathing and her every breath looked up to Jesus to take her. Even with all the pain, she knew God could redeem all of it for his glory and could use it to help a dying and a dark world that needs the light of Jesus so desperately! If she hadn't endured what she had thus far, she wouldn't be as mighty a disciple as she became because the Lord saw the bigger picture even when all she could see was dark and doom.

The Crack in the Ceiling

Anna Voskuil

There's a crack in the ceiling just like there is a crack in my brain. And when I stare long enough, I see it growing. First, a deepening chasm into the innermost part of what hides between the neurons that are shriveling and those that list toward the light of the sun, phototropism of dreams and nightmares. Mostly nightmares.

And then, I watch it spread. Radiating out in spider web projections, tendrils of darkness and sinkholes of hope. Questions of when will this be over? And reassurances of it might get worse before it gets better. But that doesn't feel like a good enough answer, so we keep searching.

Rusty razor edge of reality and twister-tumbled carnage from the inside because it's a one-way road, and the body doesn't expect to be destroyed from the inside out. Which also means, it wasn't ready for destruction from the outside in, like it usually is, because it was trying to fix a mistake. A break in the code. A flaw in the design.

And the vulnerability of the unknown strikes fear inside your chest, up into your throat so that you forget how to make sound. How to form the words that are falling into the crack, echoing as they tumble down into a place that will never be reached again.

And the fear scatters out into the extremities, so that you can't reach out to grab the tree trunk for stability. It enters the heart so you don't quite remember what it means to love or to be loved. It spins around in your lungs, like a bizarre, heavy-duty cycle on the washing machine. And it pulls apart the hemispheres of your brain. Another crack. Another fissure. Another error message on a vending machine saying, try again later.

Another shriveled, liquid nitrogen frozen flower before your physics professor pitches it against the wall, where it shatters. Pieces that superglue will never hold together again. Dust of the promise destroyed. Dust of the once living.

I once watched, frozen in place, as an entire door made of tempered glass broke, forming tiny, dull, square-like pieces, the sound of ice on the top of a pond creaking as a bird hops across it. The voice of the water vapor when it transforms into frost on the windshield of your car.

I sometimes wonder if my brain is like tempered glass. What does it mean to be fragmented into so many tiny, dull pieces? When the dullness is a deep ache instead of a stone skipped across the water. Or the whooshing of your rapid heartbeat in your ear instead of the smoothed edges of sea glass deposited as the tide goes out. Instead of the piece of worn driftwood, returning to land in the hands of a beachcomber, a different version than before, so as to better remember its life journey. What is a journey without a transformation? And what is a transformation without the journey to get there? And how much longer will the journey be?

Because when I stare at it, I see it growing—the crack in my brain. But if you watch long enough, even when your brain is screaming at you to look away, something surprising happens. Light shines through the crack. And then a hand emerges. And another hand, and another. And you are being pulled upward, out of the downward spiral, and you remember that sometimes you have to put your trust outside of yourself, especially when the darkness blankets the hope. Especially when you feel you have nothing left to give. And the gratitude fills the spaces between what once felt broken and the love fills in around it, protection from the darkness and the fear of the unknown. And as you find your voice again, you whisper, "thank you." And even though it is quiet, it can still be heard.

Thank you to all the hands that have helped me up. And thank you to all the people whose voices comforted and reassured and paused long enough to listen to mine.

Anna Voskuil writes, *"I have lived with depression for many years. I imagine it having hands, tearing my heart apart and often sending me into a spiral of sadness that is hard, though never impossible, to recover from. I have also seen the ways in which my depression has transformed into my family members' sadness as they hope for relief for me. And that awareness of their sadness is one reason why I think advocacy is important."*

To My Dearest Loved Ones

John Witcher

Being diagnosed with a severe brain illness at 20 years old was hard on family and close friends. I remember how helpless my mom felt, doing her best to make me understand that this was not my fault. I remember those long days in the hospital, when she promised it would get better, and the countless hours dad spent with me at the group home. There were so many times that I wanted to give up. Instead, I have achieved so many of my dreams. I will never forget the love and sacrifice that all of you gave, so unselfish and unconditional. Thank you from the bottom of my heart.

Sincerely,

John

Tribute to Those Who Have Supported Me on My Mental Health Journey

Kitt O'Malley

Thank you to those who have supported me over the years.

To my friends who urged me to seek help when I was a suicidal college freshman.

To the UCLA resident advisor at my dorm who found an excellent psychologist for me to see when I was in crisis.

To that UCLA psychologist who helped me combat my depressive thoughts using cognitive therapy. As I rewrote my thoughts, I rewired my brain.

To New College of California, where I received my master's in psychology and went on to become a licensed psychotherapist who worked with severely emotionally disturbed adolescents.

To the therapist that I saw in my 20s who helped me deal with my family of origin issues, even though in doing so I found myself becoming more and more depressed.

To my doctor who prescribed antidepressants when my depression became so deep at age 30 that I struggled to get out of bed.

To the friend who called my priest and my parents to let them know that I needed help when a change in antidepressant medication triggered a week of manic psychosis.

To my priest and a seminarian with bipolar disorder who visited me while I was psychotic and encouraged me to call my psychiatrist.

To the antipsychotics that quickly stopped my psychotic mania.

To my parents who flew up to help me get back on my feet and welcomed me back home.

To the psychiatrist and therapist who helped me become stable on a low dose of a new antidepressant and supportive psychotherapy.

To my now-husband, who when we started dating told me that I was the most independent woman he had ever met. I laughed, for at 31 years old I was living at my parents' home and working as a temporary file clerk.

To the advice nurse who advised that I see a psychiatrist or go to the emergency room when I described hypomanic symptoms when I was 39.

To the psychiatrists and therapists I have seen over the years since my diagnosis changed from depression to bipolar.

To the psychiatric hospital where I received excellent care.

To Fuller Seminary where I discerned that God has called me to a mental health ministry.

To the mental health community which supports each other and advocates for positive change.

To living with a sense of purpose.

Kitt O'Malley *is an author, mental health advocate, and former psychotherapist who lives with bipolar disorder. Her memoir,* Balancing Act—Writing Through a Bipolar Life, *offers hope to those living with mental illness and their loved ones.* Balancing Act *recounts Kitt's struggle with bipolar disorder, the two decades it took to receive a proper diagnosis, and how her journey gave her purpose. Kitt balanced living with bipolar* *disorder with her work as a mental health advocate and caretaker of her son and parents.*

How God Saved My Life Twice in One Year

Cindy Higgins

It was Memorial Day, 1990. I was in seventh grade. My grandparents owned a cabin in the middle of a beautiful forest in New York State. The entire family was there celebrating. Dad hitched up the tractor to the trailer and covered it in hay bales. Soon we were off.

The road kicked up some dirt as we took our ride. We were joking and singing. My youngest cousin grabbed his dad's beer and threw it over the wall of the trailer. He giggled at the look on my uncle's face as toddlers tend to do. My dad told me to jump out and get it on the way back. As he was slowing down I went to jump out but my cousin Anne (name changed) said, "I'll get it!" and went to pick up the litter.

There was a screech of tires as everyone heard a thud. A car had come around the blind corner going very fast down the normally empty road. Anne slammed into the front of the car and flew about 40 feet. Everyone jumped into action. The aunts rounded all of the kids up to get them to look away. The uncles ran to her aid. I decided to run back and get help. We were less than a quarter mile away from the cabin.

I ran about halfway when I felt myself collapsing. A car was coming near me and I waved them down. They gave me a ride the rest of the way. People looked curiously at the car of a friend who had just left the party coming back.

I jumped out of the back seat of the car. I screamed that Anne had been hit by a car. Her mother started running down the road. The friends who gave me a ride stopped her and took her to her daughter. My grandfather called 911. Eventually the only people left with nothing to do were me and my grandmother. We sat there and prayed.

Emergency services were there much faster than anyone expected. They life-flighted my cousin to the hospital where she underwent surgery. My grandmother told my family years later that she always gave a certain amount to the ambulance service in that area and she was thinking of not donating that year but something made her do it anyway. She will always be grateful for the urge to donate.

The next day I had to go back to school. No one knew if my cousin would be okay. They knew she would survive but not how normal she would be. I was very emotional. The bullies saw that. I was always picked on. Being bipolar but not diagnosed yet seemed to be a beacon for others to pick on me. The more I was told to just grow a thick skin, the more I cried. The only real friend I had on this planet was the cousin who was in the ICU.

I spent the week praying. Anne got better. The plastic surgeon took a look at her x-rays and declared that her face would be fine. Did you know that God made the face shatter on impact to protect the eyes? Her jaw was fine, so she only needed four new teeth implanted to fix her face. She broke both hips, her collar bone, and arm, and wrecked her neck. It still bothers her to this day. Years later, she would find that her peripheral vision lost a few inches. Overall, she would lead a perfectly normal life.

The thing that really stands out is what the doctor said about me. He took one look at my smaller frame and said that I would never have survived the impact. I was too short. My head would have hit the edge of the hood instead of the top of it, and I would have snapped my neck. She saved my life.

Before I knew all of these things, I just knew that my only friend was possibly dying in the hospital. The people in my class made me feel even worse. I prayed to God that things would be okay, but I seemed to get no answer. I had been suicidal for years at this point.

I decided to go to sleep. I took a bottle of medicine and downed it. I just didn't want to wake up. An hour later I was sick. I spent the entire night purging everything I had taken the day before. To this day, my parents think I only had a bad flu.

Okay, God had answered my pleas after all. I should have died. I shouldn't be here.

Finally, I got to visit Anne. She was in good spirits. They had her on pain medicine and she was healing. It took six weeks, but she was eventually moved to a regular room and then sent home in a wheelchair. I spent my summers with her because her mom was worried that she would become spoiled being an only child, so I was able to help her and play for a few months.

I told her about my guilt, and she said that there was nothing to forgive. To this day, I know that she saved my life. Many years later we would talk about that summer and a few horrible things that happened in the years that followed. We are both suicide survivors and got matching tattoos of a semicolon. Our life had a pause in it, but we are past it and will continue to live.

God saved me twice that year. I don't plan on throwing this gift away.

Cindy Higgins writes, *"I was born in the 70s as the middle child in the small city of Erie, PA. Grew up Catholic but in a family that encouraged Bible reading and asking questions. I don't remember when I gave my soul to Jesus. I just feel like he always had it. I honestly debated on becoming a nun but felt pulled to be a mom instead. Discovered I had bipolar in high school after my sister was diagnosed. It's been a bumpy road with anger management issues and projects that are only half-finished in my house. Luckily, I have a supportive and understanding husband. I am currently blessed with the perfect life: loving husband, two healthy daughters, a dog,* *cat, and enough income to pay our bills but not so much that we become lazy."*

Dear Grandpa
David Teike

Dear Grandpa,

I don't know if I'd be alive without you, but I almost certainly wouldn't have near the gratitude for the many blessings that I have without your wisdom and encouragement over the years. You have set a powerful example for me to try to be a compassionate and sober-minded person. You have made me appreciative for the gifts God has given me and grateful for the chance to live a life of purpose and happiness.

You are a humble person who leads by example, and I will never forget your words of truth, kindness, care, and encouragement. You have always been there for me and for many others. The fruit of your spiritual practice over so many years has really shown itself brightly, as I've seen your love in my and many others' lives. When I've been at my lowest and in despair, you've lifted me back up, helped me to see the blessings I had, and to live again with a grateful heart.

I couldn't have asked for a more generous and loving grandpa. I love you.

Sincerely,
Your grandson

Dear Precious Ones

Debbie Teike

Dear Precious Ones,

We are family, not a condition or set of circumstances; yet, mental health conditions create challenges for us from time to time, testing my ability to act in love toward you and myself. During times of uncertainty, I live by the Serenity Prayer to embrace acceptance, change, and surrender.

Maybe it is helpful for you to know that my journey of recovery abides in silence. Even as I am an extrovert and love community, it is in silence where I listen and experience life in all its complexity, without judgment or agenda. To be still and know that God is God and He never changes recalibrates me to a state of calm. I remember that God is the same yesterday, today, and tomorrow, even as my personal, family, or world circumstances change. God is the same when:

- Wind is taken out of my sails and knocked completely out of me;
- Questions of why, how, how long, what, when, or who dominate my thinking;
- Solutions, relief, and peace seem so unattainable;
- Well-meaning "supports" give unhelpful advice;
- Adrenaline and cortisol flow through my body demanding long walks for relief;
- Those on the streets, jailed, or lost are traumas too visible to ignore.

And God is the same when:

- Smiles send warm energy through my body;
- Responsiveness of professionals brings direction and care;

- The right medication advances purpose and connection;
- Community provides support and education;
- Sojourners unite to tackle discrimination and marginalization;
- Perseverance reminds me that I am not consumed.

Life can be complex, overwhelming, and disheartening. Therefore, my journey of recovery is often experienced in a wilderness, a place away, removed and barren. Strangely, it is in this desert-like environment where I often find fertile ground for replenishment. Here, I connect with God on a soul level. I remember that despite any condition or circumstance, God is good and gracious, slow to anger, and abounding in steadfast love. He wants the best for me and you and always provides a way out. The emotional, relational roller coaster of mental illnesses is fertile ground for replenishing parched, thirsty places in life with oasis and rest. I come as I am, weary and burdened, and I find rest.

What I know is that you matter to me. Therefore, as you suffer, I suffer. Equally so as, as you heal, I heal. But the reverse is true also: As I suffer, you suffer, and as I heal, you heal. Sometimes we heal together; sometimes we heal apart. Still, God is good all the time, and He never changes, and we find peace. I pray that you always experience this peace from God that surpasses all human understanding.

Debbie Teike, *Art of Invitation, LLC*

Hope
Dina Coughlan

Hope is something I often lost when I was navigating through a serious mental illness. I could no longer see beauty and purpose in my life. This created a sense of darkness and made me feel like a failure. My future looked grim, and I could not appreciate the many blessings that I did have. I was no longer grateful for anything because the dark cloud that hung over my head convinced me that I had been forgotten.

However, as my life slowly started to turn around, I noticed I was beginning to see things very differently. When I look back on those painful moments of desperation, I now remember that I was not alone. In fact, I was never alone. My brain just wanted me to believe that I was. I now know that even when I was in treatment facilities and on psych wards, trying to make sense of what had become of my life, I was surrounded by people who wanted to help me, people that would not give up on me. I just couldn't see it.

I believe that hope is not always present in our lives because we refuse to acknowledge the little things: a smile from a stranger, a beautiful sunny day, a hug from someone you love. Learning to have gratitude is a skill that takes a lot of practice. It takes a shift in your perception of life, seeing the glass half full instead of half empty.

When you suffer from a mental illness, the world can seem like a dark, cruel place, and the glass can appear half empty. However, I encourage you to find the beauty that is present every day because what I have come to learn is that, even in the darkness, there can be glimmers of hope.

Although my journey through life has been difficult, the struggles I faced made me who I am, and I would not change that. I have finally learned to be grateful for the small things and to embrace second chances because that is what I have been given. I am grateful to be alive. I am grateful that I get to share my story in the hope that my heartache can help someone else. I hope that the path I have carved out can light the way for someone who is lost. I am choosing to believe that the finite disappointments of life should never cause us to lose infinite hope.

"We must accept finite disappointment, but never lose infinite hope."
–Martin Luther King Jr.

Dina M. Coughlan *is a passionate mental health advocate and aspiring mental health empowerment speaker. Her passion for mental health stems from her personal lived experience, and she hopes that her story will help give others hope.*

Dear Loved Ones Living with Mental Illness

Ilona Poka

Dear Loved Ones Living with Mental Illness,
Please know that I am beyond grateful for our trip to Ireland. I don't have any regrets, and I am grateful I was with you. I always loved you, and now, I love you even more!

Remember when we were younger? You had the most adorable platinum blonde curls and your smile lit up the room! There were so many of us cousins; I remember the feeling of fun, love, and pure joy at our family get-togethers. We really did have a close, loving family.

We were a bit different from the other cousins. We lived in the same house together or right next door for quite a few years growing up. Do you remember when you used to come to Carmel and party with me and my friends on the weekends? You and I have a lot of special memories together.

It's been over 20 years since I've been in Arizona, so our connection wasn't the same as it used to be. I really am so happy to be part of making your dream come true. We shared the beauty and history of the sights. I love how you opened up to me and told me about your future dreams.

I apologize. I didn't realize that the reality of so many of our family members experiencing childhood trauma would be so hard for you to process. I wanted to let you know you weren't the only one.

I desperately wanted you to let go of the shame. It was not your fault! You did not deserve it; you did not ask for it, and you most certainly could not say no. Since I've started speaking about childhood trauma, I have found there is so much shame around it. Most people keep it a secret.

Do you remember leaving me at the Cliffs of Moher? Our routine was to get off the bus, go to the bathroom, meet in a central location, and do the tour together. I came out of the bathroom and waited and waited and waited. I wondered if you jumped off the cliff or if someone stole you. I finally saw someone from the tour, and they told me you were with them. When you finally showed up, you continuously apologized. I asked you what happened, why you left without me, and you said you didn't remember.

It was dinnertime, and I was excited about your birthday celebration. You went to get a beer at the bar and didn't come back. I ate dinner while tears ran down my face. I was sick to my stomach not knowing where you were. I called you numerous times and you didn't pick up. I banged on your hotel room door in desperation as my heart screamed that I had to find you.

We searched the hotel grounds for three hours looking for you. We watched hours of security recordings and realized you never left the building. The hotel staff finally found you. I felt beyond grateful you were safe!

I walked into the conference room, and you were sitting in the dark all by yourself. I asked you why you were doing this on your dream trip to Ireland. You said we weren't in Ireland. What do you mean we weren't in Ireland?! We had been there five days already. I was overcome with fear and anxiety.

I knew I had to call the paramedics and get you to the hospital. By the time they came, you were outside smoking. You wouldn't answer any of their questions and refused to talk to them. The paramedic called me inside and was very concerned. He said you weren't responding and there was a 30-foot drop off that balcony. They were afraid you would jump.

The paramedic asked me if I would sign to involuntarily admit you to the hospital. I felt I did not have a choice. I knew that you were not in the right state of mind, and I had to do whatever I needed to make sure you were safe.

I watched you sleep on the couch for hours in the hospital emergency room. A million questions and thoughts flooded my brain. Why is this happening to our family? Why are there so many people in our family living with mental illness? What can I do to make a difference? For you? For the rest of our family?

When I did go into your hospital room with the doctors, you did not want me there. You looked at me in disgust. I knew it wasn't you; your eyes felt empty. I felt like I was no longer seeing my cousin and wondered where the hell did he go?

I was terrified you would end up homeless in Ireland. I wasn't sure if the hospital would release you in 24 hours like they do in the States. I verified with five doctors and nurses that Ireland's law will not release you without a next-of-kin there. Only then was I okay leaving you once you were admitted into the hospital.

Please remember every decision I made was out of pure love. I wish I could take away your pain. I would hug you until the last bit of it goes away.

I wish it were that easy.

There is only one thing I can be sure of; I am going to influence the world's perception on childhood trauma and mental illness. You are one of the reasons I am so passionate about this work. You have always been like a brother to me.

I will speak the truth about our family for our family.

I love you, cousin.
Love always,
Ilona Poka

Ilona Poka *is a business consultant, professional speaker, mental fitness coach, and owner of Truth Be Told, LLC. She is also the Founder and President of Mental Illness Refined, her 501(c)3 non-profit.*

To the Residents of Group Home A

Anonymous

To the residents of Group Home A, you deserve to have a clean, safe, and up-to-date facility. You deserve to have services suited to your needs, rather than those of your service provider's need for billable hours. You see, your service providers are judged, not on the quality of care provided, but rather on the quantity. The metric is always quantity over quality.

Your care should be fully funded, so that those serving you don't have to stretch the truth to bill for your care. You also deserve to have providers who are paid enough to prevent the high turnover prevalent in community mental health. That way, you don't have to keep establishing a new level of trust with your service providers or suffer poor care while new service providers learn the job by trial and error at your expense.

You deserve a pharmacy that doesn't constantly make mistakes on your medications, without any apology or explanation. You deserve to have more access to your Rx prescribers for answers to your valid questions. For most of your fellow citizens, if their pharmacy frequently made mistakes, they would simply find a new pharmacy. But you do not have that choice; instead, you are stuck with an extremely poorly functioning pharmacy.

You deserve to have private rooms, instead of shared rooms, so that you aren't dealing with the fallout of someone else's mental health struggles on top of your own. You also deserve to have food that is sanitary and not cooked by residents who don't follow adequate personal hygiene. You also deserve to have food that is nutritious, not just whatever is cheapest because of a ridiculously low food budget.

To the mental health technicians serving this population, myself included, you deserve a work environment that is safe enough to discuss your own mental health diagnosis without having it used against you through gossip. I have a lot I could share from my own experiences, as do several others, but I am certain it would be used against me because I have witnessed firsthand others sharing theirs and it being used against them. This is a disservice to those served in the community with mental illnesses, as well as to those who serve them.

To our community at large, not being able to have loved ones admitted to the hospital or psychiatric facilities against their will, when it is clear they are a danger to themselves and others, is nothing but a lack of compassion dressed up as personal freedom. The freedom to die in the streets is no freedom at all.

Perhaps the biggest disservice is for Christian service providers who are not allowed to share their faith in Christ and the hope it provides. From my perspective, a life without Christ is hopeless. And spiritual resources, including the Bible, are real resources. A true understanding of God's Creation, Grace, could result in better medication compliance, as well as something healing for which to thank God.

Encouragement from a Carer's Heart

Kathrine Elsa

"In His time He makes all things beautiful, In His time." This is a song I sing so often to remind myself that He, God our Father, can and will make everything beautiful. This song continues, saying, "Lord, please show me every day that You are teaching me Your ways in your time."

As a carer to my only daughter, 26 years old, I draw close to the heart of God's grace, trusting Him for His heart towards her as she faces a life she did not plan to have. I have joined groups like Kay Warren's called Breathe, which encourages me to take one deep breath at a time. She further encourages me to share my mother's heart with those who cannot find hope in the middle of deep pain.

My daughter has rapid-cycling bipolar depression with psychosis. She has a life that looks different from what we all thought, but it is a life that God Himself is creating, and He is creating a beautiful one. I would like to encourage you as a carer that a journey with mental illness does not have to be hopeless and can be beautiful in its own unique way.

Here are a few words of hope and possible advice that I have found along the way.

• Ask questions and find someone who can listen and answer you. Even if it might not change the diagnosis, a listening ear always helps.
• Get out and go for walks, even if it is around the house outside.
• Take deep breaths and practice patience; this takes practice.
• Keep it in the present time and focus on something other than the past or future. It is important to find a balance in this.
• Yes, it is a fact that your loved one is struggling, but God can make a way, and He will.
• Learn to take breaks; having your own time as a carer is important.

• Quite simple, but your loved one will dance again.

• Be open and honest with yourself and your loved one.

• Sing songs of encouragement and hope, empowering yourself with grace and gentle words of love. This will spill over to those you care for daily.

• A note for the parents, it is important to have open communication and be on the same page. This helps to provide harmony within the family and ultimately helps the struggling individual to feel secure.

Always remember that the diagnosis is not your loved one's identity. They have a disorder, but they themselves are not the disorder. They are so much more. They are a unique individual with a life of hope ahead of them. They deserve love and grace. To leave you with one thought is to say that this world of mental illness does not have to carry the stigma of shame. It is okay to struggle, even as a Christian.

Walk with grace, seek, learn, listen, and love. You'll do great.

My Testimony

Larry McNabb

Editor's Note: warning—discussion of suicide.

If you or someone you know is thinking about suicide, please call 988 for the 988 Suicide and Crisis Lifeline or text the word HOME or START to 741741 for the Crisis Text Line.

Many times, I am asked why I am so passionate in suicide prevention, suicide attempt survivors, and suicide loss survivors? I do not share my complete story much, but recently a dear friend and pastor has been going through some struggles in his life, and I thought I would share some with you. Thank you for supporting me over the years and being there when I was at my worst.

On Thanksgiving Day in 1986, I heard the news that I never thought I would hear; Theresa took her life. I heard of suicide and even experienced the loss of an uncle-in-law to suicide, but I was not old enough to remember this loss in a traumatic way.

Over the years, her loss and how the small community never reached out to the family afterwards affected me and still affects me this many years later. Since that devastating loss, I went through unknown "attacks," and I did not know what they were. After a couple of years of these attacks and after different tests, I was diagnosed with transient ischemic attacks (TIAs). There were four places in my brain that these lesions appeared on an MRI/MRA. How did these mini-strokes affect me? I know there is some difficulty with my swallowing, and I have a crooked smile, as well as one side of my throat is very sensitive and the other side not much at all. A lot of the issues are not known.

In 2005 and 2006, I lost weight to where I was only 123 pounds and people at the rescue mission where I worked asked me if I was dying. I wanted to say, "Yes, but not in the way you are thinking." During this timeframe, I was really struggling to get through each day, and I cried on a daily basis. Each morning, I would cry out to the Lord, "Why did you allow me to wake up this morning?" I could not see the light in the tunnel of darkness that I was in. I did not recognize the person that was looking at me in the mirror. This went on for days, weeks, months, and into years. My wife said that if I did not get help, I would die, and I would not be around to see the milestones in my children's lives. I got help and was diagnosed with severe depression and general anxiety with panic attacks. I went through different medications and counseling, and I still take one anxiety medication.

In 2008, I attended a Kickoff Banquet for the Kentucky Suicide Prevention Group in Frankfort and I heard a heartbreaking yet hopeful story from Major General Mark Graham and his wife, Carol. This was the first time that I heard someone talking openly, honestly, about the devastating effects of suicide. I made sure that I was able to meet the Grahams afterwards to share how thankful I was for hearing their story and how it has opened a door in my life to be a voice.

On the way home, I was in tears as the Lord placed on my heart to start a Christian Survivors of Suicide Support Group. I joined KSPG immediately after this banquet, and I have not stopped being proactive and being that voice for the many that are struggling to live through another day of pain. In July 2010, I was asked to become a Certified QPR (Question, Persuade, Refer) Suicide Prevention Gatekeeper Trainer. Since then, I have had the privilege and honor to conduct over 250 Gatekeeper training sessions with a few thousand people. In May 2014, after much prayer, research, and finding the right co-facilitator, I, along with a dear friend, co-survivor of suicide loss, and strong Christian wife and mother, Kari Mulderink, started our Christian Survivors of Suicide Support Church at the First Church of Christ in Burlington.

Our group has met on the second Wednesday of each month since our start. In July 2020, in the midst of the worldwide pandemic shutdown, I became a Certified Mental Health Coach through the American Association of Christian Counselors and Light University. In December 2020, I felt the need to pursue becoming a Master Trainer with the QPR Institute. Since becoming a Master Trainer, I have had the privilege and honor of training over a couple hundred new trainers here in Kentucky. It is encouraging to see that mental health disorders, addictions, and suicide are being discussed in our community, in our churches, at the state level, federal level, and global level; there is still much work to do, and there is such a need to have more people that have a calling, a passion and desire to reach the many hurting people around us. Suicide prevention has not been around for a long period of time, so we were way behind when we first started addressing this area.

The church and our Lord Jesus the Christ is the one true hope in our world and we as Christians have to be willing to go into the darkness, the trenches, and the world to shine His light that is dying without knowing that true hope in Him.

You Share Your Body with a Beast

Anonymous

My Love,

I hope this letter finds you well. A lot of things have been going on lately that have crushed both our hearts, but I want you to know that I love you and I know that you love me. You are a man of God. You are loving, caring, and compassionate. You care about me and worry about me when you see that I am sad. You are a blessing to me. You are knowledgeable of the word of God and you look for God very closely. You pray for me before I go to work and make me breakfast and coffee every morning. You make my mornings go smoothly. You wake me up with a kiss and check on me throughout the day to make sure I am okay. You have shown me unconditional love when you help me around the house and have coffee ready when I come from work. You massage my feet and serve me food.

Something I like about you is that you are very sensitive to the pain of others and dislike those who abuse vulnerable people. When I get sick, you take care of me to the best of your ability. When I lost my cousin to cancer, you were there by my side and supported me, even though you could not find the words to say.

You are a very special man, but you share your body with a beast. This beast usually comes out when someone or something makes him angry. He is mean and vicious with his words towards me and others. He likes putting people down who do not agree with him. He hurts me with his words, and you allow him. His words are like a sword to my heart. This beast's purpose is to kill and destroy whoever steps in front of him. He knows how to devour his prey, and he uses the word of God to crush me because he knows my fears and flaws.

His power subdues you. He has a plan against me and for other people you love. He does not care about how much his words can destroy me or the pain they can cause, because his purpose is to have me bow before him and praise him.

I need you to find help getting rid of this beast so that you can stay afloat all the time and we can be happy to express our love. Would you find the help you need to get rid of this beast?

It's Not Boring! An Open Letter to My Best Friend on Our Tenth Anniversary

Martin Baker

Dear Fran,

I'm writing this sitting on the bench that's been my regular stopping/thinking/journaling place for a while now. I've had calls with you here many times and taken you along on my walks, sharing my world in photos, chat, and voice and video calls. We're 3,000 miles apart, but we still use all the tools and means available to bridge the distance and keep our friendship and lives vibrant and aligned.

Ten years ago, we'd not yet met. That was still a few days into my future and yours. (It's a constant reminder that transformational change can appear at any moment.) And then that evening came, and I posted seven words to a friend's Facebook wall. A friend who was struggling. In pain. Suicidal.

Flooding light and love into your world.

Unknown to me, you were there too, at the same time on the same Facebook wall. How my naïve words, intended to soothe our mutual friend, enraged you! Had my words been less hopelessly inadequate, you might not have been moved to respond as you did.

Sometimes, even too much love can be overwhelming.

The irony isn't lost on me. Had I shown even a little more empathy, you and I would never have met. Likewise, if I'd not dared to post on her wall at all. How easy it would have been for me to just click away. It's a scary thought. I can't imagine my life without you in it. It is upon such moments that our lives turn. Our friend isn't here to share our anniversary with us. She knew of our meeting that night on her page, though. It pleased her, I think. She is not forgotten.

You've said many times that you'd not be here if it wasn't for me. If not for us. I take you at your word, and there are no words to express what it means—how it feels—to believe you. And I do believe you. I would be here today, even if we'd never met. But the person I am—the man sitting here writing to you—did not exist ten years ago. Or perhaps he was always there, but not yet awake.

"Does anyone call you Marty?" you asked. "No," I replied. And in that moment the new me was born. I didn't save you, but we have helped each other save ourselves. To become, together and apart, who we truly are.

Most days, we meet for video calls, but today you're visiting friends on Peaks Island. Your life on the mainland is much richer, but I miss those days on Peaks. Your little house. Walks on Centennial Beach and around the island, me following along in photos, words, and the tracking app we used to use. We've come a long way since then. So much has changed, and so much hasn't. We're here for each other as much now as back in those early days. We're stronger. We have grown, in trust and in maturity. I've learned so much from and with you. I'm a better person, a better friend, for knowing you.

I was looking back over these ten years to pick out some highlights. Our first and only day together in person, in Southampton, is right up there, but there are so many more. Many of our moments and memories are private, but a good deal of our friendship has been lived out on a wider stage. I'm writing this letter, for example, with the intention of sharing it on our blog. And it is ours, even though these days it's me who provides most of the content and maintains the site itself. Pretty much everything we do in the wider mental health space is us. Teamwork makes the dream work, as they say. Our creative platform is an important part of our story and journey together.

I know there have been times when you regretted suggesting I write a book about what it's like to be friends with someone living with mental illness, but you did suggest it and I (we) did write it! As you reminded me once when I was doubting myself: "You wrote a book. A whole fucking book. Don't you give yourself credit for that?" Our book is our great endeavor and achievement. I will always be proud of that. I refer to it a lot myself, to remind me of things we got right—and things we got wrong!

Our blog. Our book. Our online presence elsewhere on social media. I'm deeply committed to them all. But they are not us. They enable us to share our story and our message of hope, but we know the stories, tips, strategies, and techniques we write about because we have lived them. Day in. Day out. Ten years. 3,653 days. (Yes, I looked it up, to be sure I had the leap years right!)

I've loved it all, Fran. Not always liked it or found it easy—we've had our share of hurt and darkness, some of it our doing, some of it not—but I've always loved being with you. I told you once, "I never don't want to be here," and that's still true, no matter what is going on for you or for me. That commitment has kept our friendship strong and endlessly reinventing itself.

The dark times and the light, the low and the high, the well and the unwell—they are all part of what we've shared and continue to share. As I'm sure I've said once or twice along the way, it's not boring being your best friend!

Thank you, Fran, for every one of the 3,653 days we've shared. Here's to the next 3,653!

Marty

Martin Baker

High Tide, Low Tide: The Caring Friend's Guide to Bipolar Disorder (Revised edition)
by Martin Baker and Fran Houston (Kingston Park Publishing, 2021).

"No one is too far away to be cared for or to care."
www.gumonmyshoe.com
www.facebook.com/GumOnMyShoe
twitter.com/GumOnMyShoeBook

Originally published at Gum on My Shoe (www.gumonmyshoe.com), May 2021.

One Last Cigarette
Mary Beth Graber

One last cigarette . . . Look in my fridge . . . Been trying to be good to our Big Kid and me, our Li'l Papas . . . Keep stocked the fresh veggies and fruits, that red pepper hummus we enjoy, fresh juices, waters and seltzer, Big Kid's iced teas, array of salad dressings, plant milks, cheeses, and her turkey slices . . . my Edy's fruit bar supply, indulgences of organic dark chocolate treats.

What sticks out in the side freezer storage . . . not mine, certainly not our Big Kid's . . . four years old already, taking up that spot. Actually moved to three different freezers, three locales in this county . . . Unopened, never had the chance to be packed meticulously as you were known for, pounding pack to palm of hand. Tight, neat, and you were famed for your rolling talents, too, LOL . . .

It never really crossed my mind to give your packs away, much less to "pinch" a puff in my many manic and despaired moments. It would've never been the same or even a proper moment. Like after a rave concert, or sitting outside, like we used to when you were in your territory, and we'd be deep in serious convo . . .

Or the times Mo threw a steak fry in OC, or the tenderloin for Easter one year, where I was drowning in the usual holiday get-together stress, as I furiously manned the grill, trying to achieve all the fam's requests from rare to medium well. And you'd come downstairs, so we'd have a smoke, and that menthol swirling relief it brought, knowing I wasn't alone or unappreciated for my lack of Steve Raichlen endeavor.

And most tragically and sorrowfully, those last times at Salty's outside in the patio, after darts. I debated handing out those two packs, during excursions downtown, just like you would do for your "brothers of the streets" that you'd hand a grit out to by Webb's after we saw Rakim at Turner Hall. You would've stood there for an hour, cutting up with them and trading stories.

And even down to your last Newp, telling me, "Ma, ya got my extra pack in your purse . . .?" smiling as wide as the night sky in full display. You'd gladly give up your last smoke and dollar for anyone in need. I just gaze at those packs, in reverence to another place and time, and leave them enshrined inside that freezer door. Reminding me of what I am missing, each and every day.

What I mourn and speak to the night skies and our moon. When your great Grandpa, our Papa Mike, passed too shortly after you were born, I missed the heady aroma of his L&Ms and Lucky Strikes. Now I yearn for the distinctive scent of those menthol-laden Newps. You tried quitting enough, but the nicotine would soothe your mind's misfiring, as it masked the brokenness from the edge of bipolar mood swings and anxiety.

Sometimes having that smoke for you, quelled it all—it meant everything. It didn't solve your world's problems, but it brought a temporary chill for the tumultuous moments. I'd gladly indulge you the Newps, versus self-medicating of alcohol or street pharma or opiates. The minefields of brain wiring gone terribly wrong aren't easily resolved by Big Pharma's standards of one pill or a cocktail of several to curb it all.

So your Newps remain the small legacy of memory, and moments in an earthly swath of survival in a trail of smoke. No one will ever again pack it like you, and nothing will ever replace your kind heart and loyal love shown to those of us you cherished, and brothers you met on your journey, even in the midst of your worst storms and endless grief. Newp smoke will never be the same, though I wake up into the dark night, and that blessed smoke fills my senses. . . I breathe in the hope and long to catch a glimpse of you, packing those packs, dragging on your Newp, laughing at life despite it all.

#OneLastCigarette Herrick Parker aka Rick aka CaRbon Lungz Forever 31

Listen to Your Soul

Michael Raymond

My name is Michael.

I am a dad, a husband, a sibling (one of six), and a very blessed fellow. If you were to look up the phrase "Brain Neurological Disorder" in an illustrated medical dictionary, you might see pictures of my family:

• a family member with bipolar I
• a nephew with depression
• a brother-in-law with clinical depression and PTSD
• a niece with schizophrenia
• a niece with Borderline Personality Disorder
• a sister-in-law with bipolar II
• a sister-in-law with Clinical Depression
• a cousin with Major Depressive Disorder and alcohol addiction
• a nephew who died from a heroin overdose as a result of untreated bipolar.

Then . . . there are successive (younger) generations with more of the same.

As with most people, I had no clue about brain neurological disorders. No clue that emotions are biochemical. No clue that we don't:

• see with our eyes
• hear with our ears
• taste with our tongues
• feel with our touch
• smell with our noses.

We do all of these things with our brain. Eyes, ears, nose, touch, and tongue are just "input portals" where we accept data from our environment. How we interpret this data and experience these inputs happens in our brain.

Having been raised by incredibly loving parents who instilled in us solid values and a strong moral core, I had no clue that brain chemistry could completely override or "swamp" our learned sense of "right" and "wrong"/"moral" or "immoral"/"fair" or "unjust." I had no clue that brain chemistry could so fundamentally alter one's perception of "reality." I had no clue that such a deep well of anger and rage could arise from solely internal sources.

No clue.

Until in psychosis, there was a stolen car. And "secret directives" nestled in radio broadcasts. And "custom messages" in license plates. And imagined offspring. And holes punched in the walls. And doors kicked out of door frames. And unintelligible words spoken at such hypersonic speed. And cowering in a fetal position, consumed by dark, for days on end. And, and, and . . .

No clue.

Some told us we were "imagining things." Some neighbors whispered "bad parenting." Some medical office staff said that we needed psychiatric care. Some doctors told us "shut up and give 'em these pills." Our favorite was "Dr. Harvard Disease" who dismissed our questions with "I got my medical degree at Harvard. Where did you get yours?"

They too, had . . . no clue.

Things began to get better with better doctors and a solid diagnosis. More than 100 titrations of meds (and counting). Non-stop reading and research, NAMI's Family to Family class, two classes with Dr. Xavier

Amador, and carefully listening, non-judgmentally, to my Loved One...all of these were key ingredients to helping me understand.

I am a blessed fellow because I have had an extraordinary opportunity to learn:

• to be more patient
• to be a better listener and observer
• to stop thinking automatically that it's "about me"
• to be less quick to judge
• to be more supportive
• to be a better Dad, husband, and partner
• to research more, to seek greater understanding
• to jump to conclusions much less quickly
• the value and importance of grieving
• to focus less on "remembering the future" (let it go. . .)
• to accept my life as it is −now−
• to be grateful for the privilege of watching my adult kids grow
• that limits and boundaries are −essential− to growth and recovery
• that when "broken," we must put our brokenness to work
• to have hope—i.e., that each of us can "do hard things"
• that life is a −long− journey that passes quickly.

Do kindnesses. Close your eyes and listen with your soul.
Find joy.

Thanks from the Bipolar Bandit

Michelle Clark

To my parents,

Waking up in a psychiatric ward at the age of 17 very manic and disoriented was horrifying. This began our family's nightmare of my life with bipolar disorder. I can't imagine the horror that you went through learning that your daughter had bipolar disorder.

In addition to seeing me that way, needing to learn more about the illness and how to help me, you had to deal with the stigma. You actually had to hide it from your friends. Some of the ones you did tell, abandoned you.

Over the years, you have had to deal with my mood swings, the awful things I said and did, and the repercussions of the manic episodes. You stayed up with me all night at times when I was depressed and had to endure my suicide attempt. There were times I got so manic, you had to travel long distances to get me admitted to the hospital.

Probably one of the worst times was when I got off the bus with a guy I had just met, bought a car, drove around, and you couldn't find me. You were able to rescue me with the help of the FBI.

To my sisters,

I am so sorry for all the things I have said and done while I was sick. I'm sorry for taking up so much of our parents' time growing up. Thanks for all the talks and letters and for visiting me in the hospital. I know seeing me manic had to have been scary for you while you were younger. Now that I am older, I am sure it is frustrating and heartbreaking to watch me endure what this illness throws at me. Thanks for being there and not giving up on me.

I am so grateful that I have been blessed with such a wonderful family.

I was engaged to someone with bipolar disorder and had to endure some of the things you endured, and I can't imagine.

This is a horrible disease to live with, but I know it has to be just as hard to watch my spirals into depression and mania.

To my husband,
We were together for a while before I told you I had a mental illness. When I told you, you had no idea what was in store, but even after a friend told you they had dated someone with bipolar disorder and to stay away, you stayed. I was working at the time and stable. Little did we know that was all going to change. You had been dealing with some depression, but had never endured a manic episode.

I am so grateful that you stayed after my manic episode that landed me in the psychiatric ward. You came to visit me every day and brought with you a love I can't describe. Thanks for sticking it out then and ever since. We have lived through some awful times together and you have been my rock.

I am so sorry for calling the police on you one time and am so glad that worked out okay because they realized I was very sick. That landed me in the hospital again and I still wonder how you have been able to stay with me, but you do. I love you for that.

To my best friend,
We met in an AOL chatroom for people with bipolar disorder. Even though you did not struggle with the disease, you wanted to learn more about it. Our friendship grew during that time, and you have been there for me ever since.

Your nonjudgmental ways and the way you have supported me over the years have helped me more than you will ever know.

We live 15 hours apart and have only met twice, but you, by far, know me the best after my family. You have endured my ups and downs and have been there for me through it all. When I came to see you, I got hypomanic, yet you were able to help me. We have spent countless hours talking on AOL and now on the phone.

You encourage me when I am depressed and help to ground me when I am manic. You treat me like I am part of your family and for that reason I can't express how much it means to have you as a friend. The most memorable times were when I was manic, and you would stay up with me and play music over the phone until I fell asleep.

To God,

Thanks for putting these people in my life and for all the times you have rescued me from myself. Thank you for giving me the opportunity to help others through my blogging and social media. Bipolar Bandit (me) is getting expressions of gratitude almost daily. You lead me to start Mental Health Advocates United and the group Advocates for People with Mental Illnesses. Although it has not accomplished all I want it to, I know that it will accomplish what you want it to.

To the medical care professionals who treat me with respect, are caring and do their job right, thanks.

To my fellow mental health advocates,

Thanks for encouraging me and allowing me to come into your lives and help you in any way I can. Thanks for all you do to help others by telling your stories; blogging; writing books; having social media sites; and participating in groups, community events, and writing letters. I especially want to thank those of you who are in contact with legislators and are actually helping fix the broken mental health system.

Thank you, Tony Roberts, for allowing me to write this and for putting this book together.

Michelle Clark writes, *"If you want to know more about bipolar disorder, other mental illnesses, read guest posts, find out more of my life story and my advocacy work, please google Bipolar Bandit to find my blog. I am on almost all the social media sites also."*

My Letter to Shawn

Sharon M. Gartrell

Dear Big Boy,

I'm writing this letter hoping that it'll not only soften my heart towards you, but help you understand how badly you've broken it. I'm so angry and resentful towards you I cringe each time you call me from jail

.

You don't understand how your actions towards me have caused us to become estranged. That means I don't want anything to do with you—for now. But because of the situation you're in, and I know you need me, I always answer your calls.

This letter is meant to heal us both. Regardless of our mental limitations and multiple diagnoses. Regardless of the pain and confusion we've caused each other and our immediate family members. Regardless of the past and the present. We must trust God, mental health personnel and each other, if we have any chance of surviving this latest fiasco.

As a Christian, Big Boy, I truly appreciate the grace of forgiveness. On several occasions I've hurt those I love. Sometimes I was mentally stable and sometimes I wasn't. But I know right from wrong, and I chose to hurt them anyway. But by God's grace they eventually forgave me. This is why we're estranged. You have deliberately hurt me so deeply it may take years for me to recover financially and emotionally, forgive and trust you again. Your father blames us both but I'm not taking the blame. The only thing I'm guilty of is loving and trusting you too much.

Love, Grandma

Sharon Gartrell writes, *"I'm a permanently disabled retired US Army veteran. I was on active duty for over 21 years. I tell everyone who listens*

that when I retired, I was totally broken. God, NAMI Memphis, and the former Memphis VA put me back together."

Editor's Note: When the editorial board read Sharon's letter, we had concerns that the trials and tribulations she experienced might cloud whatever hope she had found. So I asked her to respond to this question. "What hope have I found?" Her reply included the following.

Three things have sustained me throughout this ordeal: God, sound advice, and my NAMI training.

1. God . . . I've prayed every day for God to soften my heart and help me forgive my grandson. I've finally forgiven him.

2. God . . . put the right people in my path to help give me sound financial/emotional support/gratefulness for a better future and final outcome.

3. God . . . without the quarter of a century of knowledge, training and hope I've received from NAMI, I wouldn't be sharing this with anyone. I would probably have had him arrested. I know once my grandson is free on probation it won't be long before he's in trouble again. It's just the nature of his multiple diagnoses and his refusal to take his meds. Because of NAMI I have sympathy for him.

She continued: I just want families to realize that very often they will be forced to deal with several different types of losses/set-backs at the same time. They need to be prepared with multitudes of resources in order to cope and survive. That's what I and my grandson have done so far this year—survived. And other families can too.

Part Two: Song Lyrics & Poetry

Chapter 6. Song Lyrics

The Champ of Peer Support

City Voices

Verse 1:
City Voices, the champ of peer support
Pros who've battled demons use their past for a report
Helpin' others on their journey, real-life recovery
Our community's strong, where peers can discover

Through Peer Workers United, our virtual support group
Friendship Squad bringin' us together like a hoop
We're building friendships, empowering our minds
Fightin' back against stigma, one step at a time

Chorus:
City Voices, a true inspiration
Peers comin' together, liftin' up the nation
We're all about the fun, the laughter, and the joy
Kracking Up, PIPs, we're never coy

Verse 2:
We're bringin' humor to the struggles we all face
Kracking Up, comedians sharin' with grace
Mental health and substance use, we won't hide
Challenging stereotypes, lifting our pride

PIP's the real deal, where peers can explore
Parks, cafés, museums, we're never a bore
We're breakin' the chains, society's norm

City Voices leads the way, our peers transform

Chorus:
City Voices, a true inspiration
Peers comin' together, liftin' up the nation
We're all about the fun, the laughter, and the joy
Kracking Up, PIPs, we're never coy

Verse 3:
Spirituality's important, our minds need a break
Meditation with a monk, for wellness' sake
Silence is golden, our souls can find peace
City Voices leads the way, our stress does cease

We're an inspiring force for good, shining bright
Peers liftin' each other up, it's a beautiful sight
City Voices, we're proud to be on your team
The future is bright, recovery's the theme

Chorus:
City Voices, a true inspiration
Peers comin' together, liftin' up the nation
We're all about the fun, the laughter, and the joy
Kracking Up, PIPs, we're never coy

Outro:
City Voices, we salute you, you're the best
Peers united, we'll pass the test
Let's keep the momentum goin', the flame lit
Together we'll rise, stigma we'll outwit.

Hope
Andrew Neil

So delicate, so free
Face of an angel
A little bit of she
Makes smiles hard to strangle
She makes me high off life
Her lips are my dope
She threw away my knife
Her name is hope

Hoooooope Hooooope
Hoooooope Hooooope
Hoooooope Hooooope
Hoooooope Hooooope

It's way more than emotion
Much more than a vibe
Where teardrops meet the ocean
Where stars and us collide
It's much more than a feeling
it's something that you breathe
goes hand in hand with healing
you are what you believe

you are what you believe
you are what you believe

so Hoooope Hooooope
Hoooope Hooooope
Hoooope Hooooope
Hoooope Hooooope

fade

Andrew Neil *is considered an "outsider music artist" in the spirit of Daniel Johnston. His music and poetry reflect his struggle with bipolar 1, depression, and, more recently, his battle with Lymphoma cancer.*

Mongolia
Andrew Neil, August 2020

I know angels on a first
A first-name basis
And I can't stare at the walls too long
or else I'll see faces, faces

I want to go to Mongolia
Perhaps there I'll get holier
Holier than the Judas that I am
Holier like Mary's little lamb
Cinderella won't return my call
You've seen Mongolia, you've seen it all
You've seen it all
You've seen it all
You've seen it all

Mommy, please don't spank me
I am way, way too old
And I need a blanky
Cuz this world is so cold

So, I want to go to Mongolia
Perhaps there I'll get holier, holier

A picture says a thousand words
my scars are photogenic
and I'm best friends with all the birds
Sometimes I regret it

I want to go to Mongolia
Perhaps there I'll get holier

Holier like I'm a little kid
Holier like I awoke in a pyramid
Oh, no, face coming out of the wall
Mongolia's a dream, a dream and that is all
That is all
That is all
That is all
That is all

My Father

Kevin "Earleybird" Earley

My father
He never said
"Why bother?"
He encouraged me to try harder
Even though we've been through more drama than an opera
He always had the best advice to offer

My father
He never said
"Why bother?"
He was there Hell or high water
Even though we've been through more drama than an opera
He always had the best advice to offer

I know now the drama isn't worth the rage
You start to reflect when you reach a certain age
Thinking about how short one's life course is
Of course it's the feeling of something more than us
That supports us
When the going gets tough, divorces
And important choices to make
I'm so fortunate—no remorse
Understand where I come from and learn to respect the source—
The author
Knowing that you were never a rolling stone
Help me hold onto the globe before I could hold my own
Your character is embedded in my chromosome
I think about how I'll be alone when you're going home
At your tombstone, I'll grieve, leave flowers and kneel
But before you pass on, I'll tell you how I feel

For another hour when you're gone I'll request
Just another moment conversating with the best
 My father
He never said
"Why bother?"
He encouraged me to try harder
Even though we've been through more drama than an opera
He always had the best advice to offer

My father
He never said
"Why bother?"
He was there Hell or high water
Even though we've been through more drama than an opera
He always had the best advice to offer

I gaze into the mirror as I take your shape
My features mimic yours
Since you make mistakes
I can't
offer you anything other than thanks
For how I was raised
No one can take your place
I listen
To my dad more as I mature
I notice now I appreciate everything that you've done for
Me
you never ignored or turned words on your second son
Even if it seemed
I was done for
Willing to make sacrifices
Taught me life is
Nothing without family to confide in

Rely on

Only as strong as the weak link

Before I speak, I consult my think tank

Look before I leap

I used to live reckless, but you always came through with a positive message

That's a blessing

I'd be stupid not to recognize

You can achieve, reach whatever you set your eyes

On

My father

He never said

"Why bother?"

He encouraged me to try harder

Even though we've been through more drama than an opera

He always had the best advice to offer

 My father

He never said

"Why bother?"

He was there Hell or high water

Even though we've been through more drama than an opera

He always had the best advice to offer

Kevin "Earleybird" Earley *is a mental health advocate and hip-hop recording artist.*

"Same Time, Next Reality"

Bill Boutin

Part 1: "Never Touch the Ground"
Same words, different views
Same colors, different hues
Same numbers, never add up to four
Same players, never know the score

Same planet, different worlds
Same lines, never being heard
Same eyes, never seeing the sky
Same heart, never knowing why

When all our lives are laid bare
The truth will be found somewhere, somewhere

Same mind, different thoughts
Same play, different parts
Same mouth, never making a sound
Same spirit, never touch the ground

When all our lives are laid bare
The truth will be found somewhere, somewhere

The song "Never Touch the Ground" is based loosely on 1 Corinthians 13:12.
"For now we see only a reflection as in a mirror; then we shall see face to face. Now I know in part; then I shall know fully, even as I am fully known."

My favorite metaphor is that of the blind men and the elephant. We're all like that in a way, stumbling our way through life, and because we are different, we all bump into different parts of the elephant.

As someone who has dealt with developmental disability and mental illness my entire life, one thing I've learned is that it is difficult to deal with people with whom one is uncomfortable. It is very common to give preferential treatment to those who look, act, and think like us, and with whom we are comfortable, and to shy away from and discriminate against people who are different and make us uncomfortable.

This is why we have racism and hate groups, why some people form groups around a common cause, and why some people are always left out in the cold. People with severe mental illness often do not have the social or economic resources to form groups of solidarity as many other special interest groups.

I have seen more support on TV for stray dogs and cats than for people with severe mental illness. Many cannot afford therapy, and medication is not always enough and can have severe side effects. So many people still end up out on the street, in prison, or worse.

Much more needs to be done to help and support those least able to fend for themselves, but there is an answer.

13: "And now these three remain: faith, hope, and love. But the greatest of these is love."

Thank you.
Bill Boutin

Bill Boutin writes, *"I am a disabled retired electronics technician who has lived with an undiagnosed Autistic Spectrum Disorder and depression,* *been happily married since 1976, and continues to advocate for people with severe mental illnesses and better mental healthcare."*

Link to video:

https://www.youtube.com/watch?v=PnWcB8xokPY

C ME

Tracey Plummer

Greetings to all and welcome to life as a client, victim, participant human being not trying to fit in your world where I am not valued or equal. Fear and ignorance have cursed my path, so as I knock on doors of help or commonalities they see my illness b4 my treatment exploits. I'm so glad there r outside voices, for if I scream I'm unarmed and target practice, I'm less than human, far from mistakes—just often kept silent by senses redefined.

EYE 2 AM HERE C ME

Chapter 7. Poetry

Until We Are Reunited

Catherine J. Rippee-Hanson

My sister and I thought we were strong.
Though burdened with a heavy wrong.
We lost our brother to injury and disease,
Leaving us with bittersweet memories.

We tried to fix it, to make it right.
So much love and hope in sight;
But darkness would not be denied.
And his life . . . the world would not abide.

Schizophrenia . . . was his last undoing.
Making his world wild and confusing;
And though we tried to keep him safe,
He turned away, lost in life's dark maze.

Homelessness was his final fate.
The streets . . . his home; there's no debate.
Our hearts were broken, tears were shed.
Before the end when he was dead.

Our brother's death is sad and tragic.
A simple illness, but too late for magic.
His soul departed from this world.
Leaving us unraveled, thoughts unfurled.

We grieved in sadness; we kept some hope.

Remembering our brother, trying to cope.
We clung to hope, as a beacon of light;
In honor of our brother, each day and night.
He had a life of love and a life of pain.
The bravery of his journey we'll sustain.
From his shining light, we'll never be apart.
For he will always be with us in our hearts.

We will keep on honoring him and his memory.
Until we are all reunited in eternity.

For the Weary

Claire Graber

For the weary. . .

This song is for me and you
When skies are not blue,
I'm here to remind you
That the sun will
Warm your face again

Just put
One foot before the other,
Moment by moment,
And soon you'll be looking back
And will see how far
That you have come

We will dream of a blue sky day,
Where laughter warms our souls.
We will dream of a blue sky day,
Feeling love to the tips of our toes.
We will dream of a blue sky day,
And that will get us through.

Close your eyes and remember that those blue sky days are coming, dear
one.

To the One Losing Hope

Claire Graber

To the one losing hope,

I see your fear, I see your pain,
I see your tears and all the hurt.
You've carried it all for too many days.
I want to remind you that we're going to:

Hope anyways—even when it makes no sense.
We're going to hope anyways—even when we're asking God, "Where are you?"
Hope anyways—even in the face of fear.
Hope anyways—because deep down inside
We know God will be right here.

I see your strength is gone, too weary to push on.
The darkness that you're in is too heavy.
Let me be your light, I'll carry hope for you,
And remind you on this day that we are going to:

Pray anyways—with faith that God will hear.
Hope anyways—through days of suffering.
We are going to hope anyway and that will be our strength.
We'll hold the hope to light each other's ways.

Yes, I'll hold the hope that will light your way.

Claire Graber *leads a successful life as a teacher while also living with a bipolar, anxiety, and OCD diagnosis. It is important to know that we are* *not alone on our journeys and that leading healthy and thriving lives is not only possible, it is attainable.*

Out of Chaos Comes Art

Colleen Wells

Once dubbed manic-depression,
bipolar disorder is a potent malady,
that wreaks havoc, making the ordered
brain disorderly, a broken puzzle.

Of the psychiatric disorders
in the DSM-IV,
it is a machine gun.

Rapid-firing tongues,
Sadness engulfed in inertia,
psychosis destroying marriages,
leaving children
addled in fear.

A friend of mine who
shares the affliction
streaked through his yard
like a white, hot comet.

Lithium, Lorazepam, Loxapine,
Wellbutrin, Depakote, Haldol,
Mellaril, Seroquel, Abilify.

And don't forget the Prozac.

I've swallowed them all
to regulate my moods.

Genetic or environmental factors?

The uncertainty belies the certainty
that without them,
some of the greatest writing
would be missing:
Sylvia Plath
bled poetry in the blue hours
before dawn, then stuck
her head in the oven.
Two orphaned children
left in her wake,
one to wonder,
another to follow suit.

Hemingway was silenced with a gun,
leaving behind his stark, limpid prose
and a family
to pick up the pieces
like gathered river rocks
that started as sand.

Narrative arcs,
incomplete.

Stranger's Got a Gun

My family doctor prescribes Amitriptyline, but I'm still not right.
A recurring thought tells me traveling to Florida
will make it better. I spend my graduation money
on a plane ticket.

There I do some things uncharacteristic of me
like walking onto a dock and inviting myself to
go deep-sea fishing with a group of strangers.
I reel in a huge Kingfish but have to throw it back
due to regulations.

After the fishing expedition, one of the strangers gives me
a ride back to my condo. I talk him into buying
me a six-pack because I am underage.

While he's inside the gas station, I open his glove box, find a gun.
It's black and not that small. I want to pick it up,
but instinct stops me.

When the stranger drops me off, he orders me to go
right inside, and be careful with the beer.
He knows something about me is off.
There's something not right about him, either.
I feel like telling him to be careful with the gun,
but instinct stops me.

Summertime and the Livin' Is Almost Easy

Collen Wells

In the summers, we go to the lake cottage for long
periods of time. We can have one paper grocery sack
for packing our clothes, and I'm not allowed
to talk too much during the drive, because my stepdad
doesn't like it, especially when I pretend
my fingers are people and start chatting with them.

At the lake, I sit by the water and read under big, old trees
whose roots are never thirsty, cuz' they're so close to the lake
for a sip. My friends are the characters in my books:
Runaway Ralph, Ramona and Beezus,
Amelia Bedelia, Charlie Bucket, and Nancy Drew,
depending on my age.

At night when our parents take the boat to their friends
who live across the lake, we sneak bread slathered with
sugar and cinnamon. My brother climbs the rafters
like a stealthy cat, and the older kids tell me ghost stories
outside in the dark.

Someone is always on the lookout for the glowing lights of the boat,
and for a while I feel like I'm part of something, but then we see the tell-
tale orange and scatter to our bunk beds, because we know we'd get in
trouble for still being up. My heart thumps as I get in fake sleep mode.
My heart hopes our parents will go out again soon.

Colleen Wells *uses writing as a way of healing. She believes in the value
of sharing her lived experiences with mental illness so those touched by it
can know they are not alone.*

My Witness

Gina Ciaccia

Without my witness at my side
When my illness took me for a ride
Nobody would
Believe ME
I would be gaslit
Nobody would
See ME
They would only see
A disease
Not a person
And there's nothing worse than
So-called healers who won't recognize
My identity

But my witness, SHE makes them see
When I'm treated like an "IT"
And not a "ME"
SHE shows them who I am
SHE opens their minds
They're closed up with doors slammed
SHE's known ME for so long
SHE wants ME healed without the pain prolonged

But who is the one who never wants me to suffer?
Who else could it be aside from my MOTHER?

The Beast Within

Heather N. Croas

Anger flowing through me like a river of rage coursing in my veins
Trying so hard to control and conceal the pain
Destruction and violence plague my thoughts
The images overpowering and I feel so lost

The Beast has awoken and rattles against his cage
Fighting for control over the rage
Looking around at all the pain I've caused
He sits inside sharpening his claws, ready to strike without a moment of pause

Anger flowing through me like a river of rage coursing through my veins
Trying so hard to control and conceal the pain
Unsure of what I'm feeling leading to the sea of confusion
Leading down the path of delusions

Need a way to tame the Beast
Or find a way to regain the control at least
His will is strong, but mine is stronger
Just need to hold out a little longer

The river is slowing to a trickle of frustration
Need to remain focused with my wavering concentration
The Beast is losing his hold
And finally I'm starting to regain control

The Maze

Heather N. Croas

Lost and confused, trying to find my way through this maze
Searching for the hope that seems all the craze
My mind is so jumbled and entangled
At times it feels like I'm being strangled

Strangled by my fears
As I fight to hold back the tears
I don't want to die
But at times it's just too hard to stay alive

Yet I still continue to strive in my search for hope
Looking everywhere for new ways to cope
My world was shattered the day you went away
And I miss you more and more each and every day
You were my one and only, the reason I could breathe
And all I want now is for this pain to ease

They say what I'm thinking is the coward's choice
But right now, it feels like I've lost my voice
Strangled by the pain inside me
Trampled by all the crap from my history

You gave my life purpose and direction
And I miss all your love, kindness, and unending affection
Looking around, I can see the way things should have been
But this is done and without you the future feels so wrong

Looking for something, I don't know what
Doing my best to pull out of this rut

Wading through the seas of anger and confusion
Trying so hard to find a solution
Hard to imagine my future without you in it
When life feels so empty while I'm stuck in this pit

Tired of fighting a losing battle in my head
Walking through life in a suit of lead
The pain, anger, and frustration weighing me down
Looking for a way out before I drown
But all I'm seeing right now is the pain I've caused
From the anger I've spewed without taking pause
To consider all the ones I loved and cared about
Before I started to scream and shout

Pushed people away when I needed them to stay
Too stubborn or stupid to realize they could help me find the way
Don't understand why I put so much resistance
When really what I seek is some assistance

I know there are those who want to help me out of this mess
So maybe it's time to confess
I can't do this alone no matter how hard I've tried
But I'm afraid to let my guard down and allow myself to cry and finally
say goodbye

Heather Croas writes, *"Both of [these poems] were written while I was hospitalized at an inpatient psych hospital in 2010 following a suicide attempt. It was actually the third hospital stay in three months following the attempt and they were written as a way to communicate to the staff what was going on inside of my head.*

The Shower
Heidi Franke

He called in for a shower after being alone on the streets for a week. Or
had it been a month?

Is that time enough
to get dirty?

She could turn him away
like her father's sister
might have and did.

From time to time.

The decision depended on how many times in a week,
month, or year
he would show up without a call.

Without knowing he still existed.

Somehow, his presence and
absence
were a mixed blessing.
His presence was like a merry-go-round
that goes against the earth's pull.

Like a brazen thorn
stuck into your shoe.
Unpredictable.

Vacuum-like.
Sucking all the dirty things in.

Taking everything in its sight
and power. Making
everything contort
to his reality.

Where he and only he resides.

Would she open the door for him?
What she does know
is that she might risk speaking
in a bright, happy voice
of a mother
so gladsome to see her son.

Welcoming him in.
Rather than turning him away
because of his inconvenience. Grief is inconvenient.
That is one thing she knows. The other thing, her love has no limits.

The Letter
John Witcher

It was in a box, labeled 1942
Looking at the picture, I thought that she was you
There was a little shop, on the outskirts of town
It was there she bought her wedding gown

One day she got a letter
It said he wasn't coming home
PFC Allen, may his soul never roam
He loved your mama, just like you do
Two hearts bound together
Forever, through and through

The ashes of a rose
Like her heart, didn't bloom
She put the letter in a box, and hid it in this room
Many went fighting, in that awful war
Never coming back to the love they adore

One day she got a letter
It said he wasn't coming home
PFC Allen, may his soul never roam
He loved your mama, just like you do
Two hearts bound together
Forever, through and through

Now you know the story
Of how their love began, two young hearts, together
Walking, hand in hand
Never take for granted, the ones you adore
Just like this letter, love them evermore

One day she got a letter

"The Letter" comes from Human Nature
Published by: John Witcher
Publisher: Amazon
Date of Publication: August 14th, 2016

The Plight of Lady Manic

Katie R. Dale

Lady Manic, she was known as, to the shrewd and cunning Mister.
Sir Madness, her unmatched suitor, wouldn't dare resist her.
She played to his schemes, his subtle plans enthralled her.
Soon, according to Sir Madness, only he could call her.

Flirting with a master of irresistible temptations,
She woke to twirling thoughts and tantalizing elations.
Once he lifted her too high, she panicked at the height,
She braved the quickening sensations amidst the fright.

At first glance it was glee in anyone's unwitting sight,
Until it was too late to do anything but fall from the flight.
Perhaps she was naïve, overzealous and of youth,
Perhaps he was too devious for her to discern the truth.

Whichever way it was, it was now in hindsight, error,
The affection they once shared was now a twisted terror.
Depths of loathing and sorrow crawled out from the pit of Hell,
In shrouds of darkness, they came moaning, cleverly cast like a spell.

Misery appeared to trade the place euphoria had been,
It seemed the day turned into night without her knowing when.
For nights came for days and try as she might will then,
No amount of pulling by her bootstraps could she rise again.

Now the words fled her mind and mouth where joy once filled,
Purpose left her spirit, whose strength none could rebuild.
Confusion mounted its cavalry, crafted artillery from its guild,
Here the war on her psyche ambushed, her sanity, all but killed.

In this infamous lion's lair, she knew of One before who'd gone ahead,
The sacrifice who died to pay the ransom on her head.
She surged her strength to call upon the name of Him once dead,
"Give me Your life, You paid my price! Redeem my life instead!"

The only One, calling on her from birth, swiftly came,
The test was passed, and she could leave the dungeon of her shame.
Alas, Sir Madness could not call on her, he had no viable claim,
Since all along she was betrothed to Lord of all Lords—Jesus, His name.

The deception that bewitched her could no longer advise,
Since she set her sights on nothing but her truthful Savior's eyes.
Victory preceded Him, overcoming Sir Madness and his lies,
And Lady Manic was no longer known as Manic, but as Wise.

I Only Had One Brother to Love Me All His Life

Linda (Rippee) Privatte

I only had one brother to love me all his life.

No one knew what was to come, to cause such despair and strife.

Until his 20s he was a handsome, kind, funny, loyal, and charming man.

An accident, a traumatic brain injury, losing his eyes . . . was not part of our plan.

His broken bones healed up using bolts, rods, wires, and metal plates.

A few years later, the true tragedy would come and the diagnosis we came to hate.

He would survive over 60 surgeries with help from our family.

We prayed about the blindness, thinking that it was his tragedy.

We could not have imagined a disease that our laws would not treat.

They would however, gladly, lead him to live and die out on the street.

Almost 16 years I followed him and every time I cried.

I loved my brother dearly, but I knew that he knew I tried.

I sat with my arms around him, on curbs, in bushes, wherever he would be.

I thought that I could change things . . . if I could only make others see.

I took to him life necessities and fought bravely to tell others about his pain.

They still refused to treat him . . . why he did not deserve it, I cannot explain.

He was locked in his mind by a serious brain disorder speaking for him.

Lack of insight prevented him from seeing his illness and already his life was grim.

My brother had now indeed become a broken, mangled man in our hometown.

His community and family "stood up" to help, but our laws told us, "stand down!"

The pain and anguish was too much and it brought our family to our knees.
No matter how many speeches made . . . no one would answer our pleas.
They would say the laws were the only thing to blame.
Then they would have the family carry all the shame.

We couldn't give up, we couldn't let it go; it didn't matter they kept saying, "NO!"
They wanted him to harm others or himself . . . that is what he needed to show!
I asked them to see what was right in front of their eyes.
Their only response was rolled eyes and heavy sighs.
So I told them I'd make sure that they all knew his story and his name.
I'd make sure our country knew our outdated laws were to blame!
We began fighting a battle that seemed more like a war . . .
It was his treatment and life that we were fighting for.

I promised to tell his story till the end, until that last day.
Telling the truth to the unknowing public was the only way!
His story was unbelievable and so . . . we had to make it clear.
We told his story thousands of times, falling on every deaf ear.
I told them in every speech he would die out on their street.
Where and when will our laws and love find a place to meet?
The day his story ended . . . was the day I feared would come.
Our war was lost and mattered not to some.

I told Mom that her only son might be going to die.
"Again? Are you sure?" as she began to cry.
"No, I can't be sure, Mom. This is what the doctors say."
She quietly said, "Okay," as if this happened every day.

Mom carried her grief as she watched her son suffer so.

Waiting . . . watching for the day that he'd really have to go.

Many times our family grieved, throughout all the years.

Still the pain was never any easier as that day came near.

Thinking of the past as he lay there dying.

Thinking of what could have been, unable to stop crying.

After he drew his last breath I leaned down and kissed his forehead.

With the weight of all society . . . "I'm sorry Mark, I'm so sorry" was all I said.

I only had one brother to love me all his life.

Now you know what we knew . . . the cause of such despair and strife.

God, I Don't Know
Martha Hackenberger

God, I don't know what to say,
what to do, to think, to pray;
how to live from day to day,
how to trust, how to obey.

God, I don't know how to feel,
how to act on what is real,
how to hope when wounds won't heal,
how to cope while lacking zeal.

God, I don't know how to breathe,
how to know what to believe,
how to stay, yet yearn to leave,
how to joy with all I grieve.

Shackled, chained, and iron-bound,
Anxiety and fear surround,
Freedom, future: only found
Hugging prostrate Holy Ground.

Be Proud

Mazie Malone

Be proud
Stand tall
Surrender
Unlike everyone else
Be yourself
Your presence matters
In so many ways
I hope you share
If you dare
How life brought you here
Tragedy & triumph
Crushing grief
Defiance
Show me your scars jagged & rough
Speak of the grace that saved you
And the strength it took to continue
Living in pain and fear
I am so glad you are here!!!

Mazie Malone *is a poet residing in Northern California. She is passionate about alleviating the suffering of families and their loved ones afflicted by Serious Mental Illness through education, advocacy, and support.*

When the Days Get Dark

Meghan Ricks

When the days get dark, you are my light.
Thank you for loving me the way that I am.

Replanting Lives—A Prayer

Nancy Boucher

This is a prayer that I wrote for our son, and try to pass along to other families . . . it is in the beginning of my second book, Replanting Lives Uprooted by Mental Illness, A Practical Guide for Families. (The cover is one of my son's poignant drawings that he labeled and called "earth wrecker.")

a prayer
today
may your suffering be blanketed with your family's love
you are not alone
your family walks in love beside you
even when you do not see
your voice
your song
weak or strong
it does not matter

I waited until the sky was
perfect blue with billowy clouds
then plucked a cloud just right for you
to rest upon

I waited for a summer breeze
then caught it in my breath to blow into the space that surrounds you

we all saw a storm approaching
we joined hands to hold it back
you are not alone
your family walks in love beside you
even when you do not see

I grew some flowers filled with sweet scent
picked the blooms when they came
then wove them into a cocoon to give you time to recover

your father cooked all day with love and made an amazing meal
to nourish you

take our hands
we will not bite
courage of heart will let you see
that we have always been here
with you

we made a balm from plants we grew
may it soothe your troubled brow
today
may your suffering be blanketed with your family's love
you are not alone
we are here beside you
even when you do not see
your voice
your song
weak or strong
it does not matter

Twenty-four years ago **Nancy Boucher's** *youngest son got sick with a serious mental illness and her family's life as they knew it veered off course. They were catapulted into a wilderness that they were not equipped to navigate. There they landed, bereft with anguish and helplessness about how to support their son who was so sick and how to support their family who were falling apart. Nancy retired from teaching four years early and became a student again—seeking to learn what might help ease the suffering for all of us in our family. It has been an arduous journey. She* *has written three books about her family's experiences and learning in an effort to reach out to others on this path—to lessen isolation and prejudice, and to share both pragmatic tools and hope. Both of her sons have contributed to these three books:* Getting My Night Vision; Replanting Lives Uprooted by Mental Illness: A Practical Guide for Families; and Defusing the Mental Illness Crisis Triangle: Safety Procedures for Families to Follow During Crises at Home.

Without a Trace

Susan Getka

Dear Tim,
The search for you continues
in my deepest thoughts & dreams
But again & again I wake up
to reality
You did go missing, dear brother
You were found too late
some of you had already
melted into the Earth
You were in heaven so immediately, I'm sure
carried lovingly on wings of angels
Flood waters swept you to your resting place
Your faith endured even though
your fingerprints were gone
as well as your glasses & shoes
after 4 days in the water
But your green lanyard & house key stayed with you
& your shirt I remember seeing you in
that last morning
A branch caught your shirt sleeve
Did you reach for it or was it a chance meeting?
Mercifully, that tree branch kept you nearby &
as the floodwaters receded, you were placed
on rocks & earth
gently & carefully
Mother Nature

I'll always be looking for you, Tim
my beautiful brother
shopping for your special snacks,

Taster's Choice, your favorite instant coffee &
your dollar store t-shirts whose label
helped the coroner identify your remains
a spoonful of sugar. . .
I'll always be searching, Tim,
for your kindness through suffering
to lead me to be
a better helper for others,
kinder towards others
until I see you again.

Love,
Sue & Hershey

"There's no amount of training that can prepare you for what people are
capable of doing to each other."
–Anthony LaPaglia as Jack Malone
Without a Trace

Caring*Taking
Tony Brewer

Eighty-seven ceiling tiles
without moving my eyes
Four blades in a windless fan
when in you walk
What
Too hot for you
this lamplight dusk?
Too humid for my shirt
against the cleaner
cooler pillow side
you turn it to
Didn't ask
for the glass of water
you hold
three-quarters full

*

That chair
under you all day
misses the shape of you
in bed at night
Yes easier
to breathe this heat
sitting up
Light leaving
What
I was imagining
percentages
coming true

Waiting on a threshold
Drinking the water
down to half

Do-It-Yourself

Tony Brewer

I'm building a girl in my backyard,
from rusty nails and rat poison
and other things I found in the attic
Mother says I shouldn't play with.
Father helps me with the power tools,
but he frowns when I roll the spare tire from his car.
He had used roller skates when he built his girl.
Everything was smaller back then.
Girls didn't fall apart like they do nowadays.
He says it was easy, fun.
You'd go to the store for a quart of milk, bread, eggs,
a girl —
or you and your friends cruising the streets,
Big Bopper growling "Chantilly Lace,"
scraping change together
to buy a girl for the night.

Mother doesn't approve
of building girls at all —
would rather I buy one instead.
She says they're worth the money,
they last much longer,
and they have better manners.
They go to church and wear long dresses
and know which fork to use with their salad.

My friends laugh at me
standing in the backyard,
welding goggles and asbestos gloves.
They think the latest model off the assembly line

painted and wrapped and talking like all the others
can make them happy—
can satisfy them.
My girl will be different
and I'm piecing her together as I go:
Mom's old toaster that always burnt the bread,
Dad's crooked 7 iron,
Grandma's photo album,
her red feather boa,
her ancient phonograph horn.
She won't be beautiful at all —
not like the cover of Cosmo
or that little number I took to prom.
But I'll never trade her in,
never set her by the roadside
For Sale
or toss her back in the attic
and buy a new and improved.

I watch Mom and Dad
buying a new car
just as the old one is getting broken in,
putting Grandma in a nursing home
because she can't understand them anymore.
They worry about me late at night —
early in the morning.
He thinks I'm getting carried away.
She thinks if I'd just get a job
I'd have enough money.

It's hard for them
to hold on to something
imperfect.

The spot welder keeps them at bay
and the ball-peen hammer
drowns out their voices.

Great Carelessness Must Never Be Taken

Tony Brewer

Approach the nest at an angle
for he guards the eggs
with serpentine intensity
They are not his but
he believes his life depends
on their safety until they hatch
into beautiful gifts
His beautiful gifts unrecognized
Anyone approaching head-on
will be snapped at and
sneaking up makes you a predator
and if you must speak
it makes the sound of eggshells
stepped on so gingerly
impossible not to shatter to bits

Injection Site
Tony Brewer

We got a flag because
he'd been in the service
but had to order it
from the casket catalog
Packing up his unused needles
like a dead soldier's locker
to ship home to Mom
waiting in the empty
house she's made over
carpets curtains darker woodwork stain
everything but his La-Z boy
I hear him sleeping in it now
needles bound for diabetics
in some other state
I learned too late to matter
I was not the kind of enemy
grunts defeat but
the adversarial construct
industries create to justify
martial law other big sticks
Dad fought unseen enemies
he took to the grave
I armed him with
a knife of his I stole
ticked away back in his casket
It's terrifying how
a family can change
in mere moments months
Styrofoam peanuts to protect
syringes and lancets all

a-hammering at his heart
as I discover what I can
get by without in this world
is of course addressed
to Gainesville, Florida,
the length of time I spend
with his clothes and watch
before I wash off his DNA
and wear them every day
is my opt-out of acknowledgment
for my gift I claim
the shirts and jackets
recently smelled of him
tape down corrugated edges
these castoffs spare ammo
delivered to another empty weapon

Lake Effects

Tony Brewer

In the morning things will be different
that first one he's missing

The counter full of coffee cups
and small clean plates in stacks
unused for all this finger food
friends close by brought that first night
The news as sudden as his illness short

Toward the lake great gray factories
silent for decades puff clouds of snow
and everyone hurrying in the iron work
but this morning a calm couch
is refuge from the Post-it list
of tasks she cannot forget: one
in the bathroom, one in the kitchen

None here safe as December ducks
on some sunny pond far away
Their ripples finally crash like waves
upon the icy landlocked beach

He's gone vibrates among the unused tines
as the disarray snaps into focus
and before her slightly less calm
sits a tall son patiently urging
himself to mourn later

He takes her unknowing hand
There is much work to be done

Working Through It
Tony Brewer

I dreamed we were on a cruise
but I was the seductive bartender

Our problems were obvious before this
and I make what you want

We were dirt poor and saved years
for this trip where I work
while you drink

The movements of the ship are imperceptible
and there are too many people
We are only alone in our stateroom
I sneak to after my shift

It is a short dream
a bridge from one odd unremembered
moment to the next

It is meaningless except my memory of it
We hated cruises though we'd never gone on one
We have been split for 15 years
I cannot now recall what came before
and what came after blurs and blurs
right up to this clear awakened present

Tony Brewer *is a poet and audio artist from Bloomington, Indiana. He performs spoken word widely and is author of nine books. He frequently collaborates with the Electroacoustical Poetical Society as well as the* *experimental audio collective Urban Deer Record Co. More at http://www.tonybrewer71.blogspot.com*

Out With the Old

Vanessa Jackson

High as a kite.
Free as a bird.
Light as a feather.
We will do this together.
No longer alone.
Let them cast their stone.
I know who I am.
I know where I have been.
Is out of the ashes!
The truth is, the catch is,
We are All the same.
EveryOne is to blame.
For the conditions we live in.
We just have to give in.
To the calls of our hearts.
Saying we need a brand new start.
Trust in yourself.
There is no One else.
Believe in yourself.
Have faith like someone else.
Who came before you.
And left you the plan.
To keep on seeking and knocking
No! Banging at the door.
Help me Father.
I long to know You more!
And so He comes, just like She says.
Waking you up.
Bringing You back from the dead.
Little by little.

Step by step.
The old you seems to slip away.
The old ways gone.
Made way for new.
The person inside.
You never knew.
Now you wonder why you were gone so long.
And how it is, you could have been so wrong.
About many things you thought you knew.
Now You know, you did not have a clue.
About what really matters.
And Whose life you live.
Finding out you were always His.
Her offspring.
His seed.
Her reproductive Reed.
A personality full of sensuality.
A version of His everlasting love.
His toe, Her face, His ever loving grace.
Now let me tell you this.
Each and every One of you are His kids.
I can tell you and say it in many ways.
Create a rhyme for every time.
Put simply, Her creation and His life.
Her Spirit.
You are His wife!

Vanessa Jackson writes, *"I am a lover of a God I have a personal relationship with and am eternally grateful for the spiritual changes I have and will continue to go through. Thank you for reading."*